THE SCIENCE OF THE EMOTIONS

THE SCIENCE OF THE EMOTIONS

BY

BHAGAVAN DAS

GYAN

Published by

GYAN

Gyan Publishing House
5, Ansari Road
Daryaganj, New Delhi-110002
Phone: 011-47034999, 9811692060
E-mail: books@gyanbooks.com

Distribution Network
gyanbooks.com
India, USA, Canada, UK, Australia

ISBN: 978-93-6208-384-5 (PB)
First Published, 1900

2nd Impression 2024

Printed at: Gyan Press, Delhi.

THE SCIENCE OF THE EMOTIONS
Author: BHAGAVAN DAS

THE SCIENCE
OF
THE EMOTIONS

BY

BHAGAVÁN DÁS, M.A.

London and Benares
Theosophical Publishing Society
1900

INSCRIBED

TO

ANNIE BESANT,

BY WHOSE WISH AND UNDER WHOSE GUIDANCE

THIS WORK WAS WRITTEN.

Learn to look intelligently into the hearts of men. Regard most earnestly your own heart. . . . Regard the constantly changing and moving life which surrounds you, for it is formed by the hearts of men; and as you learn to understand their constitution and meaning, you will by degrees be able to read the larger word of life.—*Light on the Path.*

CONTENTS.

CONTENTS.

FOREWORD.

किं ते धनेन किमु बंधुभिस्ते
किं ते दारैः पुत्रक यो मरिष्यसि ।
आत्मानमन्विच्छ गुहां प्रविष्टम्
पितामहास्ते क्व गताः पिता च ॥

Mahábhárata.

"What hast thou to do with riches? what hast thou to do with kin? how shall wives bestand thee, son! that shalt surely die? Seek the Átman, that which lieth hidden in the cave. Where are gone thy father, and the fathers of thy father?"

Such was the teaching, still more ancient, addressed by an ancient Indian father to an ancient Indian son—addressed by Vyása to his son Shuka — Shuka who grew to be greater even than his great father. And such used to be the origin of Philosophy in olden India.

विवेकवैराग्यवतो बोध एव महोदयः। "He that possesseth discrimination (between the Passing and the Eternal), he in whom desire (for the fleeting) hath died away, his is the great gain of wisdom." So Vishvámitra assured Ráma when leading him to Vasiṣhṭha for the teachings embodied in the "Mahá-Ramáyana." From वैराग्य, *vairágya* — from the ceasing of desire — from विवेक *viveka* — from the discrimination which sees that all objects of desire are limited and fleeting, and, therefore, painful — from these alone, but from these without fail, proceeds the बोध, *Bodha*, the Knowledge, the true Philosophy that grasps that which is not limited, not fleeting, and, therefore, not painful.

Thus ancient Philosophy took its rise in the relation of the Jíva[1] to those two constant companions of its life, the two sole guides of all its action—Pleasure and Pain, Joy and Sorrow, Happiness and Misery, Gladness and Sadness. It set a distinct aim before itself, the aim of relieving pain—that pain, that master pain, of doubt, uncertainty, and hopelessness, which, while it lasts, poisons the very roots of life, and throws all other pains, even the pains of positive loss and physical torture, into the shade. And

[1] The separated Self.

it proceeded straight from pain to the cause of pain, and thence to the remedy.

That Philosophy remains and will remain true for ever, but it has to be modelled into ever new forms to meet the needs of the ever changing races of humanity.

The more advanced races and classes of the present humanity have, in the march of evolution, come to the stage where "Intelligence" (the fifth principle, the distinguishing characteristic of the Âryans, the fifth race, the पंचजना: *panchajanâh*) is attaining its highest development. In order to reach its proper perfection, it has become in the beginning exaggerated beyond its due proportion. The immediate result is that even as itself—being in reality only a means in the service of that essential and deepest nature of the Jíva, *viz.*, Desire-Emotion, for and towards the securing of proper action for the fulfilment of that Desire-Emotion, —has taken up the position of end and thrown Emotion into the background, so, in all departments of the life of those modern advanced

time than the performance of that business; there is more supervision and inspection than work to be supervised and inspected; more writing than reading; more newspapers than news. So much precise and elaborate calculation is made, that it very often ends in defeating its own purpose by not making sufficient allowance for contingencies which are beyond calculation; a thousand, a hundred thousand men are sacrificed, by competition, to ensure the success of one man; the outer is looked at far more than the inner; governments, systems of administration, diplomacies, and policies come sincerely to be believed to be far greater and more important than the people and their simple well-being, for which only they exist; cities come to be greater than fields; town-life than country-life; a fine dress than a beautiful physique; the author than the book; the writer than the reader non-productive labour than productive labour; luxuries than honest industries; "glorious war" than "inglorious peace"; an ever-growing, an ever more unwieldy statute book than never-changing good men; an education that cultivates the outside, that gives external polish, that fits for struggling with others and profiting surreptitiously and plausibly at their expense, than a training which opens the inner man, and fits him for real peace with Self and peace with others, fits him to suffer wrong rather than do it. The culmination point of this high growth of error is reached when professional philosophers assert that the object of Philosophy is not Truth, but the pursuit of Truth; that the latter has far greater interest than the former.

Such are the inevitable consequences, at a certain stage, of the onward process of evolution; and they need not be regretted, since they have their proper place in the story of man. Without passing through them the Jíva would remain wanting in a very necessary experience.

But it must *pass through* them, and not remain immersed in those quagmires.

That intelligence, developing and expanding, should, even through exaggeration, reach perfection in wisdom, and not descend into the deep imperfection of cunning, it has to become Self-intelligence, and not only Self-intelligence, but All-Self-intelligence; it has to understand its own true nature, in one Jíva and in all Jívas.

To know man is the noblest—and whether noblest or not is the most urgently needed—qualification of man. Philosophy in this sense is the very highest of sciences, and has always been thus regarded in the East. And it has been pursued too in the West, but the reasons which, as just said, have there very often made philosophers find greater interest in the pursuit of Truth than in Truth, have confined attention largely to the Psychology of the Senses and the Intellect—the means of cognition—on the one hand, and to the discussion of Ethics—the principle of action—on the other.

The energising motive of both the Senses and the Intellect — the Desire-nature, the Emotion-nature, of man, his रागद्वेषम् *Rága-Dveṣham*, love-hate, has not received proper attention, nor has even that which it has received been fruitful of good and true results. Because of the initial error in selecting the starting-point of investigation, these two branches of Philosophy to which have been given so much time and labour have also remained untraced to their true roots.

Not till the springs of Pleasure and Pain are reached and plumbed, not till there is earnest sympathy of search between the questioner and the teacher, the student and the science, not till mere superficial and cynical moods of asking are cast away, not till the human heart is pierced as deeply as that of Shuka by vairágya such as that which underlies the ancient counsel given to him by his father Vyása—not until then shall the pure waters of true Knowledge and

Philosophy and deep consolation flow forth in a constant, sure, and never-failing stream.

For students thus touched with vairágya, and yet by necessity of circumstance belonging to and dominated by the prevailingly intellectual nature of the present races, this booklet is written; it treats of the Desire-nature of man, his Emotions, in the way, as far as may be, of the usual books on the science of Psychology, and attempts to lead those students on from the science of the Emotions to that highest science which deals with the very roots of life, with the ultimate principles of the Universe, the science of Peace.

May the little book serve its appointed purpose, under the blessings of those who are the Guardians and the prayers of those who are the Servants of Humanity.

PRELIMINARY NOTE.

THE ANALYSIS AND THE CLASSIFICATION OF THE EMOTIONS.

The latest result of the discussions in the West on the subject of the Emotions seems to be that each Emotion is something *sui generis*, that an organic connection between Emotion and Emotion is not traceable, that it is vain to try to reduce any one Emotion into terms of any other, and that a genuine, unarbitrary, and inartificial classification of these mental phenomena is impossible.[1]

It seems to some that this result is not final, that a true classification of the Emotions is possible, that an organic connection and an evolution of the complex from the simple are traceable amongst them. Valuable hints on the subject are to be found in Vátsyáyana's *Commentary on the Nyáya Sútras of Gautama* also in the works of other Indian Schools of Philosophy, and notably in the various works of Sáhitya, the science of Poetry and Rhetoric,

[1] See Ribot: *The Psychology of the Emotions*, Chap. x.

which bulk largely in Sanskrit literature, beginning with Bharata's *Nátya-Shástra*.

An attempt is, therefore, made here to lay before the philosophical public a very brief sketch of a scheme of the Emotions based on the assumption that they can be analysed, and, therefore, classified. This is done with a view to invite further discussion of this vitally important branch of Psychology. If a true science of the Emotions could be discovered, the art of consciously, deliberately, and purposefully cultivating the higher and better ones and weeding out the lower and the evil would become a possibility—with what beneficent ultimate consequences to humanity is at present matter more for poetical and religious imagination than for sober matter-of-fact expectation. Yet, there is no doubt that the theory and method of education would, even immediately, benefit greatly from such a science.

In view of these possibilities it is very desirable that any conclusion as to the impos-

presented themselves more or less definitely to an enquirer. Defects will be found especially in the use of the names of the less common Emotions, inaccuracies in the appraisement of the true values of them, which are inevitable when a foreign tongue is used. But if, notwithstanding such shortcomings, there should appear to be any substantial truth in them, abler hands will naturally take these outlines up, and supply the necessary amplifications, corrections, and details of illustration.

The method that has been followed is, as it could not but be under the circumstances, introspective and analytical. But this should not be understood to mean anything that goes against the fact—which lies behind all that is written here—that Self and Not-Self, Spirit and Matter, Pratyagátmá (Purusha), and Múla-prakṛiti, are always inseparable, that changes of "Mind" always accompany and correspond with changes of "Matter," and *vice versa.*[1] What is meant is only this, that here the one series of changes is considered more prominently than the other.

[1] James's and Lange's theories of the physiological origin of Emotions represent the one exaggerated extreme of this truth, as the older theories of the emotional origin of certain physiological changes represent the other.

CHAPTER I.

THE FACTORS OF EMOTION.

(*a*) Beginning then with the simple, and proceeding thence to the more complex, as is the approved method of all exposition, we find as the first and most elementary factor of life—the SELF.

It is no mistake to call the Self the most elementary factor. It is not possible to analyse it into anything which is simpler, more intelligible, more directly present to a living being. The Self, towards itself, combines in one ever-present mood — conscious or sub-conscious, deliberate or otherwise, but ever-present all the same—the three moods in which it looks towards the world outside it, the three moods of cognition, emotion, and action. These three moods are distinct in reference to the outer world. But the mood of the Self towards itself may indifferently be styled Self-consciousness (Self-knowledge, Self-cognition), or Self-feeling (Self-desire), or Self-assertion. To say that "we think before and after," that the life of the Self is made up of memories and expectations, is only to describe what accompanies it, what is involved *with* rather than *in* the Self and Self-consciousness: to say this is not to analyse the Self into any simpler constituent elements; it is not to show that the Self is made up, composed, of any elements which do not already presuppose it. It is the same with other endeavours to analyse the Self. A myriad doubts may cluster *about* it; there is not possible any doubt as *to* it.

But it is no use entering into further discussion on this point here. That discussion properly belongs to Metaphysic as distinguished from Psychology. It is enough for present purposes to say that the Self is the indispensable first basis of life, even though it may be doubted that it is simple. In the words of Váchaspati-Mishra in his Commentary (the *Bhámati*) on the *Shárîraka - Bháshya* of Shankarácharya नहि कश्चित् संदिग्धे अहम् वा नाऽहम् वेति । "None doubts, am I or am I not."

(*b*) Indispensable to Life in the same degree is the *Not-Self*, something other than Self. When the world which is cognised and desired and acted on as something different from the Self has been named the Not-Self, the last name has been given to it. It cannot be reduced any further, even as Self cannot be. Life is a relation in which the two indispensable factors are the Self and the Not-Self. In this relation appear the states which are dealt with next.

(*c*) Equally universally known and recognised, and perhaps equally impossible to analyse into anything simpler, are Pleasure and Pain, the two Feelings proper, which, in alternation, are the constant accompaniments of the Self. (Most psychologists assume a third state of the Self—Indifference.) Vátsyáyana also expressly espouses this view, and he names the third state मोह: *mohah*—by etymology meaning, apparently, "unconsciousness." But, to say the least, it is doubtful whether analysis will not always show in every specific case that "indifference" means only a very mild degree either of Pleasure or of Pain. For the purposes of this essay it is not absolutely necessary to determine whether there is such a third state or not. It is enough to be sure that the two states of Pleasure and Pain exist.

It was said just now that these two are "perhaps equally impossible to analyse into anything simpler." This was said in order to avoid opening up another discussion not immediately relevant at this stage. But it may be mentioned in passing that a slight but elucidative reduction of these into terms of the Self appears to be possible; and a statement thereof may be found to be unavoidable later on. The full discussion, however, belongs to the Metaphysic of the Self.

(*d*) The next step is that with Pleasure goes Attraction—Liking; with Pain, Repulsion—Dislike. The mood of the Self towards, its attitude, its condition in the presence of, that which causes it Pleasure is Desire, Attraction, Liking, the wish to be nearer. The opposite mood, towards that which causes Pain, is the mood of Aversion, Dislike, the wish to be more distant. Generally speaking, in the most comprehensive sense of the terms used, it is true that whatever pleases is liked, whatever pains is disliked; and the primary consequences of Pleasure and Pain are, on the one hand, the desire to take in, to absorb, to embrace, or, on the other hand, to throw out, to push away, to repel, the object causing the pleasure or the pain respectively. This desire to be united with or separated from an object is Love (राग, *raga*) or Hate (द्वेष, *dveṣha*).

CHAPTER II.

THE ESSENTIAL NATURE OF EMOTION.

At this stage it will be noticed that there is a subtle but radical difference between the oriental philosopher's view of the nature of Emotion and that taken by the western philosopher, especially since the time of Kant. The latter view divides mental functions into three kinds: (1) Cognition, (2) Emotion, and (3) Volition; it includes desire *with* if not exactly *in* volition; it regards Emotions, such as anger, terror, love, &c., as distinct from desires, and as *kinds* of the feelings of Pleasure and Pain; and it holds the distinction between volition and action to be something very definite.

The oriental philosopher, on the other hand, appears to regard all these **वृत्तयः** *vṛittayah* (moods, functions), which are usually called Emotions in western Philosophy, as *Desires.* His classification of the phenomena of consciousness is into (1) Cognition—ज्ञानं, *Gnyánam*; (2) Desire—इच्छा, *Ichchá*; and (3) Action—क्रिया, *Kriyá*. जीवो जानाति, इच्छति, यतते। "Man knows, desires, and endeavours," *i.e.*, acts.

It may seem awkward at first sight to say that "action" is a mental function. In order to compare the two views it is necessary to accept the western use of the word "mind" as covering the three fundamental aspects or modes of the Self, as being, in fact, equivalent to "consciousness." The word "mind" should perhaps properly be restricted to the Self as knowing, and should not include the Self as feeling, or the Self as acting, while the word "consciousness" should include the three, each of the three being a mode of consciousness. But using the word "mind" as it is used in western Psychology, the eastern psychologist substitutes "action" for "volition" in the threefold division, and "desire" for "emotion." When we say that action, *i.e.* physical action, is a mental function, we mean that the inner nature of action is essentially a function of consciousness, that the living physical body is something which is a part of consciousness, indeed, it may be said, is itself an expression of consciousness. Just as no western psychologist hesitates to say that cognition is unmistakably mental, though it is possible only by means of the sensory organs to begin with, and has for object always material things in the ultimate analysis; just as he regards desire as something mental though possible only in a material body, and for material objects also in the ultimate analysis; so to the Indian philosopher action too is mental, though using a material body to bring about material changes in the final analysis.

There should be nothing surprising in these conclusions, for they have been established over and over again by the deepest and most independent thought. Vátsyáyana of India says प्रत्यक्षपराणि प्रमाणानि or प्रत्यक्षपरा प्रमितिः *i.e.*, certain knowledge, assurance, indefeasible cognition, has its finality, its basis, its perfection, its all, in Pratyaksha, sensation, direct cognition, direct perception. Mill, of England, says the same thing. And Hegel, of Germany, also says emphatically. "Everything is in sensation." For sensation is not the mere vibration in physical cells answering to a stimulus from without; in its pure psychological significance it is the first, the earliest, response of the Self to the Not-Self, the answer of consciousness to an external impact, that first modification of consciousness wherein Self and Not-Self are both present. This is obviously primary, for the Self must sense ere it can think or act.

Briefly, then, the distinction between volition and action is not made in the East as it is made in the West. प्रयत्न *Prayatna*, endeavour, is one of the attributes of the mind with the Naiyáyika philosopher, as is volition with the occidental. But *Prayatna* means more than volition: it is effort, not only in imagination, but in actual action. Those western psychologists who are inclined to take the view that volition is only the strongest desire, or the resultant of all desires at any particular moment, that it is *desire passing into action*, come very close to the Indian view.[1]

To put the matter in other words: Indian thought recognises the general distinction of, and the special opposition between, Self and Not-Self; but it does not favour the distinction between Self and mind and matter, or only mind and matter, such as is made in most western philosophy. Most Indian schools of philosophy follow the lead of the Vedánta in holding Buddhi and Manas, to be जड *jada* (unconscious—part of Not-Self). The truth underlying this view seems to be that what is known as Manas, the mind, arises only when the Self comes into contact with the Not-Self:

---

[1] Schopenhauer uses the word "Will" in the sense of "Desire."

the Self cognizing the Not-Self has as its organ mind.

It may be noted that the Indian three-fold classification of the phenomena of consciousness takes no account of the "Feelings of Pleasure and Pain," whereas the western classification includes them, though vaguely. The reason for this may partially appear from the discussion which will be entered into later as to the nature of Pleasure or Pain.

But the following statement—though scarcely likely to convey much meaning at this stage—may be made as being rather needed here, and also in the hope of giving a clue to the full explanation in connection with the later discussion.

That reason appears to be that "Pleasure" and "Pain" are *degrees* of the Self, rather than *forms* or *aspects* of it. It may be said, by somewhat stretching the use of words, that they are connected with the "substance," the "bulk" of the Self, rather than with its "form"; and as such they pervade and overhang all the life of the Self and its manifestation in the three *forms* or *aspects* of cognition, desire, and action.

Perhaps the following considerations may explain how the western view as to the nature of Emotions came to prevail.

Every one of the Emotions is either pleasurable or painful. The two aspects of Emotion in this general fact, viz., of Emotion as Emotion, and of Emotion as pleasurable or painful, are not usually or carefully discriminated in ordinary life, and attention has not been sufficiently directed to the distinction existing between them. Nor, indeed, does there appear to have been made any systematic or successful attempt to exhaustively and truly class the Emotions under the two heads of Pleasurable and Painful. Even this would probably have given a clue to the true nature of Emotion. What is generally and broadly observed is that particular situations in life arouse particular Emotions, pleasurable or painful. The truth here is that the Emotions are *desires* either to perpetuate the situation if pleasurable, or to escape out of it if painful; and the prospective fulfilment of the desire or the defeat thereof, in expectation and imagination, gives the foretaste of the corresponding Pleasure or Pain, and makes the pleasurableness or painfulness of the total mood. The Emotion thus begins in, and looks back to, a feeling of positive Pleasure or Pain, and looks forward to, and ends in, a possible Pleasure or Pain. These various elements are, however, blended together in ordinary consciousness so closely that unless a distinction is deliberately looked for it easily escapes notice, and each Emotion comes, as it has come, to be regarded as something unanalysable and *sui generis*.

But it should be noted closely and carefully that the Desire-Emotion specialised by the immediately surrounding circumstances of the particular situation is one thing, and the Pleasure or Pain specialised by its correspondence with such Desire-Emotion is another thing.

The later parts of the book may, perhaps, succeed in throwing more light upon this point, and make it plainer.

The above brief examination of the difference between the two views of the nature of Emotion, and how it came to arise, gives the clue to the proper classification of the varieties of Emotion; for on the Indian view it becomes possible and permissible to analyse and thereby classify Desire-Emotions.

The precise meanings of Desire and Cognition and Action; how the one consciousness of the Self breaks up into these forms and why; what the precise relation is between Desire on the one hand and Pleasure and Pain on the other; how the two, (i.) Desire, and (ii.) Pleasure and Pain, can be characterised with reference to each other in such a manner as to avoid definition in a circle; which precedes and which succeeds in the first instance, or whether there is no such first instance, and it is impossible to trace an ultimate precedence and succession, as in the case of the seed and the plant;—these are questions which are not hopeless, but should find treatment and solution in the Metaphysic of the Self and the Not-Self, of Space, and Time, and Motion.

For our present purpose let us take as the starting-point for our study, after the foregoing cursory discussion, that Emotions are Desires, and that the two elementary Desires are: i., the Desire to unite with an object that causes Pleasure; and ii., the Desire to separate from an object which causes Pain; in other words, Attraction and Repulsion, Like and Dislike, Love and Hate, or any other pair of names that may seem best.

In the hope of suggesting a possibly fruitful line of thought, and therefore even at the risk of being supposed to propound a mere verbal quibble, it may be stated here that Love, the desire to unite with something else, implies the consciousness of the possibility of such union, and that its full significance is this: an instinctive, ingrained, inherent preception by each individual Self, each Jívátmá, of its essential underlying unity, oneness (एकता *Eka-tá*) with all other Jívátmás, all other Selves; unity in the Being of the All-Self, the Supreme Self, the Pratyagátmá; and the consequently inevitable endeavour of these individual Selves, these fragments of the one Self, to break through the walls separating each from each—the walls that have disrupted the original "one" into the "many"—and thus merge into each other and reform the single whole. So too the full significance of Hate is the instinctive perception by each Self —*now identified* with a larger or smaller mass of the Not-Self, of Múlaprakṛiti, matter — of the non-identity, the inherent separateness, the manyness (नानात्व *nánátva*) of each Not-Self, each atom of Múlaprakṛiti, from every other atom, every other Not-Self, and its endeavour to maintain such separate existence at all costs and by all means.

CHAPTER III.

THE PRINCIPAL EMOTIONS AND THEIR ELEMENTS.

We have said that Attraction and Repulsion, Like and Dislike, Love and Hate, are the primary, basic Desire-Emotions. A rapid recapitulation of the facts involved in these may be useful; and in the course of the recapitulation, an important and necessary addition will be made to the general idea of the nature of Emotion outlined in the preceding chapter.

"Attraction," "Like," "Love" implies:—

i. That contact, association, with another object has at some time been found empirically to result in pleasure. Though the general question as to which precedes the other, desire or pleasure, is incapable of solution here, there seems to be sufficient ground for assuming, for our present purpose, that, confining ourselves to a single life of a human being, the first experience of the new-born infant is a general, vague, undefined craving, want, desire for nourishment, for something that will keep up its life. The mother's milk supplies this want, and from that moment of positive, definite pleasure, the indefinite want is specialised into a distinct desire, a liking for the milk. Therefore it does not appear to be incorrect to say generally that "Attraction" implies a previously experienced pleasure.

ii. It also implies that there is a memory of this past fact, and

iii. That there is expectation of a similar pleasure occurring in the future under similar circumstances. Lastly,

iv. That there is in consequence a desire for repeated contact, for association, for union with that object. But that

iv. (*a*) While contact and association are possible an absolute union is impossible. Where "union" (and here too it is after all only apparent) is possible, as between the feeder and the food, the desire remains a *desire* only. It does not advance into the condition of an emotion proper, which is the attitude of one *Jíva* towards another *Jíva*, between which two Jívas an absolute union is impossible, though an ever closer approach to it *is* possible, and is being always made in the world-process. An Emotion is, thus, a desire *plus* the cognition involved in the attitude of one Jíva towards another.

As to what the real truth is of the apparently complete union between feeder and food; as to whether there is any truth in the distinction of animate and inanimate; as to how subjects, Jívas, becoming embodied in Upádhis, sheaths, masses of the Not-Self, become objects to each other; as to how and why each Jíva atom carries in its very being and constitution both the powers of attraction and repulsion, whereby there results the impossibility of an absolute union or an absolute separation—these are questions for the Metaphysic of the Jívátmá.

But the facts enumerated above as being implied in all Emotion are based on that Metaphysic; and it has to be mastered if they are to be understood in their entirety. These same facts, studied in the light of that Metaphysic, exclusively and truly explain the process of the growth of Individuality, of Ahamkára, step by step, through the various "bodies," "sheaths," "sharíras," "koshas," of Vedántic and Theosophical literature.

To return; the expected pleasure pictured in imagination—imagination and expectation represent only slightly different aspects of the same mental process—interblending with the desire, and the two together constituting a special mental mood, have, as before stated, been taken generally as one Emotion-feeling, rather than one Emotion-desire; attention having been more taken up with and fixed by the pleasure-element than the desire-element.

Feelings proper are, as already stated, only Pleasure and Pain, which are special degrees of Self-cognition, Self-feeling, Self-realisation, Self-consciousness.

The very word Emotion indicates that in the beginning, at the time the word was formed, the desire-element and the idea of the motion and action consequent on desire were more prominently and truly present before the minds of the men who first framed and used the word. Emotion is only a form of motion; motion *towards* an object, or *away from* it, in the mind, is Emotion.

Let us see now how this simple primary form of Emotion (defined as a desire *plus* an intellectual cognition), this movement *towards* an object, Attraction, Like, Love, differentiates into and evolves the more complex forms, as between human being and human being.

i. Attraction—*plus* the consciousness of the equality with one's Self of the attractive object, is Affection, or Love proper.

ii. Attraction—*plus* the consciousness of the

superiority to one's Self of the attractive object, is Reverence.

iii. Attraction—*plus* the consciousness of the inferiority to one's Self of the attractive object, is Benevolence.

How the distinctions of equality, superiority, and inferiority arose between Self and Self, Jíva and Jíva; how indeed the Peace of the Supreme was broken up into the dual of Pleasure and Pain; how in its motionlessness there appeared Attraction and Repulsion what the true meaning of Power, Force, Ability to cause or undergo a change, Ability to attract or to repel, is; how the One and the Many arose side by side in the Distinctionless;—for a solution of these intimately connected and intensely absorbing questions—without a satisfactory solution of which indeed final satisfaction is not possible—for such solution Metaphysic proper must again be referred to. For we are dealing here with relations between the existing and not with origins.

But it seems desirable and possible also at this place to make an effort to explain what the meaning is of these cognitional elements, the consciousness of equality, superiority, and inferiority, which play such an important part in the structure and development of the Emotions, and which are indeed the sole cause of their differentiation from the homogeneity of Love or Hate into the heterogeneousness of numberless kinds, shades, and grades. A physical analogy will serve our purpose completely. Given attraction between two magnets properly placed, that which moves the other towards itself without itself displaying motion would be called the more powerful magnet; while the other would as clearly be called the less powerful. But if the two should, both of them, move towards each other simultaneously and meet half-way, they would be called equal in power. The case is exactly the same between Jíva and Jíva. Given attraction between two Jívas, that which moves towards the other first is so far the inferior; that which moves the other towards itself first, is in that space and time the superior. If the two should move towards each other simultaneously then they are equal.

The same idea may be expressed in other words, thus: Love is the desire for union with the object loved, and therefore ever tends to bring subject and object to one level in order that they may unite and become one. The fact that one Jíva possesses a quality which meets a want in another Jíva lies at the root of their mutual attraction; it furnishes the common ground, the possibility of unity, of coming together, between them. Where these wants and other corresponding supplies are both about equally divided between two Jívas, so that each has wants that the other supplies, we may speak of them as equal; for each is inferior to the other in his wants, superior to the other in his corresponding supplies, and these deficiencies and superfluities existing on both sides, their sums balance each other. Exchange will go on till deficiencies and superfluities alike have disappeared. Where the wants of one Jíva are his distinguishing characteristic in his relation to another Jíva whose distinguishing characteristic is his power to supply those wants, we may speak of them as inferior and superior. Here also the action of Love gradually leads to equalisation, as the superior fills up the deficiencies of the inferior, thus lifting him to his own level and making union possible.

Repulsion, Dislike, Hate, may be analysed in exactly the same manner as Attraction, and yields the three principal sub-divisions of

i. Anger—In the case of the equality of the object of it;

ii. Fear—In the case of the superiority of the object of it;

iii. Pride—In the case of the inferiority of the object of it.

All mental moods whatever which are by general consensus called Emotions—as also many which are not so-called but which are in truth well deserving of being so-called—will, on close analysis, be found (*a*) either to fall under one or other of these two triplets which cover the six principal Emotions of humanity; or, (*b*) to be compounds consisting of elements taken from both. The mental moods which are not generally recognised as Emotions fail to be so recognised only because they are not so intense as the others, and are accompanied with a less degree of general excitement—expansion or contraction—of the system (speaking physiologically) and of the Self (speaking psychologically). In them the desire-element which stamps a mental mood as Emotion and induces urgently to action is weak, sometimes so weak as to be imperceptible; while the cognitional, the intellectual element is strong and prominent. In the ordinary books on Psychology they are either not treated of at all, or are vaguely and loosely referred to the department of the intellect exclusively. Examples of them will appear later on.

CHAPTER IV.

THE SUB-DIVISIONS OF THE PRINCIPAL EMOTIONS.

Let us now try to follow out the complex developments of these comparatively simple Emotions with special reference to the desire-aspect of them.

i. The attraction felt to an equal is the desire for union with the attractive object by means of equal reciprocation. By *reciprocation*, because an absolute union is possible only by the dissolution of the forms enshrining and making separate the Jívas, of the forms through and in which only Love (as well as Hate) between Jíva and Jíva becomes possible By *equal* reciprocation, because the two termini of the nexus, the two parties to the relation, being equal, neither has any net surplus to give away to the other, neither suffers from any net deficiency which could be supplied from the stock of the other. Only an exchange is possible. And the more varied the things exchanged, the more constant and rapid the intercourse, the more complete and all-sided the gratification of the requirements of each by the other, the greater, the more perfect the Love. But always only the *more* perfect—always only a greater and greater approximation to perfection; never the *perfect*, for that implies absolute identification where-with Love ceases. And hence the mysterious (because unanalysed), never-gratified, ever-vague, ever more inward-receding longings of Love, the sex-love especially of early youth.

The degree of reciprocation, and the objects in regard to which it takes place, are the sources of the sub-division of this head of Emotion into many minor heads.

Desire for union, for harmony, by reciprocation in merely social matters, between persons superficially acquainted, and mostly confined to the avoidance on either side of acts which would make the other feel inferior and small, and the performance of such as would promote and strengthen the feeling of equality—such reciprocation corresponds to that mental mood which is indicated by the word Politeness. Making way for and salutation of each other are instances of the physical manifestation of this mood.

A higher decree of reciprocation in matters deeper than those involved in ordinary social intercourse, underlies the Emotion of Friendship. A Saṁskrit verse sums up the features of

Friendship, rather prosaically no doubt, but in a way which very aptly illustrates and confirms the truth of the analysis which lies at the root of the present classification:

भुंक्ते भोजयते चैव गुह्यं वक्ति शृणोति च ।
ददाति प्रतिगृह्णाति षड्विधं मित्रलक्षणम् ॥

"Sixfold is the characteristic of the friend: he gives and receives presents, confides and is entrusted with secrets, entertains and is entertained at feasts."

The prominent physical manifestation is the hand-shake and the arm-in-arm.

The desire for union by means of the highest degree of reciprocation possible between human beings, possible in perfection only between two human beings of the opposite sexes at the present stage of evolution, of reciprocation covering all the departments of human life, is Love proper. The physical manifestation is the embrace, the constant association, and the living together of family-life.

ii. Attraction towards a superior where the superiority is slight is Respect. Respect with regard to some one quality or more, where the object of that Respect is inferior in other qualities, becomes Esteem for the whole man. The physical accompaniment is the प्रणाम *praṇáma*, the bow.

Where the superiority is greater the Emotion becomes Reverence, Veneration, finding expression in "kneeling for a blessing," "touching the feet," "bending."

Where it is complete, as that of one who is regarded as the Creator, it becomes Worship, Adoration, appearing in "prostration before the Lord."

In the above three cases the desire for union—which desire inevitably takes shape as imitation leading to equalisation, absolute union being impossible, as said before, without breaking up the material forms or Upádhis— is the desire for equalisation by *receiving* from the superior, as is unmistakably manifest in the upturned hand of prayer in the case of worship, and is present, though not so expressly, in the other forms also.

The stages through which a worshipper passes in his worship show the equalising power of Love in a remarkable way. At first he is chiefly conscious of the immense superiority of the object of his worship, and his longing for union finds expression in the wish to submit himself to guidance to efface his difference: "Thy will be done, O Lord, not mine." This substitution of the will of another for his own produces in him a likeness to the object of worship, assimilating his own nature to that of the higher one, until he reaches the point where he is no longer conscious of the existence of two wills, one of which is subordinated to the other, and where the expression of his Emotion is: "Thy will and mine, O Lord, are one." This is the cry of perfect Love, in which worship is replaced by ecstasy, by a sense of union achieved. The impulse of Self-surrender which is found in the worshipper is not due to any feeling on his part that he has something to give which is wanted by, or can supply a want in, the object of worship; but is rather a complete throwing away of everything which might stand in the way of the free flowing in of the superfluity of the superior, so that by the reception of that superfluity he may be raised to the level where union becomes possible by equality, by identity, of nature. It should be noted here that worship is made with one of two ends, (i.) the one seeks to secure and prays for some gain to the Self of the worshipper as separate from all other Selves; (ii.) the other seeks the good of that Self only as united and one with all other Selves. In the former case the Self-surrender (which constitutes Devotion and is the common accompaniment of worship and generally the indispensable condition of its fruitfulness and success), however apparently and outwardly complete and unreserved, is in reality conditioned and reserved by the primary and ever-internally-present aim of the particular benefit desired. This is what is known as सकाम तपः *Sakáma Tapah*, worship or asceticism or sacrifice with an object, with a wish to gain, to get some particular thing or power. On this path lies the danger of which it is said, "Even great ones fall back." In the other case, where the Self is surrendered to the Ideal of Self-Sacrifice, to the Íshvara who is the Lord and the Incarnation of Sacrifice, and only to Him and to those who are His representatives in high offices of Self-sacrifice, however openly reserved and conditioned with reason the surrender may be, yet it only is in reality internally complete, for that reason itself is universal and all-embracing, and not a limited and limiting desire for the benefit of one only. Such surrender, dictated and governed by universal Reason, is the true and permanent Devotion which is instanced in the case of the Puráṇic Ṛishis whose Tapas is जगद्धितार्थं (*Jagad-dhit-árthaṃ*), for the good of the world; whereas the other Devotion is only temporary, as shown in the case of the Daityas and Asúras, who performed sacrifice only till they had obtained the boons of power that they had craved all along, and then threw devotion and penance to the winds.

From the above it will appear that while the Emotion of Worship pure and simple is "the desire for equalisation by receiving, Devotion is something more than this; it will be treated of again later.

iii. Attraction towards an inferior is Kindness, having as physical manifestation the smile of welcome, encouraging approach by assuring a kindly response, and meaning, here, the sense of "superiority," of "moreness" that is willing to give, is accompanied by the desire to give. (The various meanings of "smile" and "laughter" will be discussed later. The smile referred to here is of course not the same as the smile of self-complacence or irony.)

Attraction in a greater degree towards an inferior, is Tenderness—wherein the physical manifestations are more prominent, more intense, passing into caress.

Lastly, it is Pity proper, and Compassion, whereof tears are the first physical expression, tears that mean the overflow in gift of the surplus of the greater, even earlier than the outstretched and downward turning palm of giving.

In these three sub-divisions of Benevolence the realisation of the desire for union, *i.e.* for equalisation, is sought by the superior by means of giving to the inferior from his own excess, and so bringing him up to his own level. And the acceptance by the worshipped of the worshipper's first humble sacrifice, by the mother of service from her son, by the benefactor of a mark of gratitude from him to whom he has done good, is not a refutation of the fact that Benevolence is "giving." It only means the gracious accord of equality to him who was erstwhile so helpless and so helped. (*Vide* the analysis of Devotion, later on.)

Notice here that the tendency on the side of Attraction is to culminate in the equality-union of Love though relations might and very often do begin with inferiority on the one side and superiority on the other. The reverse is the case on the other side of feeling, where Repulsion is the motor-power. The ways of virtue starting from two points, compassion and humility, meet in Love. The way of vice starting from anger, diverges endlessly into scorn and fear. But notice also that Love, in the abstract, is neither selfish nor unselfish. It is the coming together of two equals, neither of whom *in the end* gains anything from the other: it is there the very climax and the end of virtue. So too Hate, in the abstract, is neither selfish nor unselfish. It is the going apart of two equals, neither of whom *at the beginning* has taken anything—but *will* begin to try to take all—from the other: and it is thus *the beginning* of vice.

As Love is the desire for union with the

object loved by equalisation, by reciprocation, so is Hate the desire for separation from the object hated by differentiation, by inequalisation. And as Love between human being and human being is not compatible with complete identification of either party with the other, so neither is Hate compatible with total suppression or annihilation of either.

At first sight it might seem that complete separation is best secured only by such annihilation, and it is true that in its pure nakedness the desire constituting Hate would be the desire for complete annihilation of the object hated; but this form of the desire is inevitably changed by the necessity of the conditions under which alone the mutual play of the Self and the Not-Self is possible. The case of Love is the same. The desire of Love is the desire for complete identification; but the desire can never be fulfilled, except by the disappearance of Love with the disappearance of its object.

Such absence of Love and of Hate, absence of movement, absence of the one and the many, absence of the abstract and the concrete, absence of Pratyagátmá and Múlaprakṛiti, belongs to the Absolute, the Parabrahm, the Paramátmá. But the discussion of that question belongs to Metaphysic, as also of the intimately-connected question—which takes its rise directly from the problem stated in the preceding paragraph—whether Moksha having a commencement has an end also or not. It would be unending if complete identification into one of those which were two were possible. Otherwise, however close the approximation, however long even the appearance of identification in certain exalted states, there will be an end and a re-disruption and the beginning of another kalpa.

The result of these considerations is that it appears that Hate proper cries: "I wish mine enemy had a hundred lives, so I might slay him over and over again;" that Hate is as insatiable as Love; for with annihilation of its object it itself dies.

The sub-divisions of the primary emotion of Repulsion, Hate, Dislike, are exactly analogous to the sub-divisions of the opposite emotion.

i. The Repulsion causing separation by inequalisation between two parties that are actually equal is, in the preliminary degree, Rudeness, Brusqueness, even Reserve and Chillness in a certain sense. The physical manifestation is "keeping off," "mutual distance," "turning the cold shoulder."

At those stages of human evolution, in those times and places, in those races, in which the *separated* Self and intelligence are strongly developed, this mood of Reserve, of "mind your own business," and "keep your distance," this absence of "gush," and suppression of "maudlinness" or "effusiveness" or "fussiness" —as the opposite mood is described by a sometimes exaggerated contempt—is most marked. Its real nature is so little understood that it is often regarded with some pride, as a manly virtue in itself, apart from any special reasons or circumstances.

In the next higher degree the desire for separation becomes Anger proper, Enmity, Hostility. The physical manifestation is "preparation to strike down the other," "exchange of abuse, or blows," amongst simple unrefined natures where the physique prevails over the mind; and amongst the so-called cultured and refined and complex-minded, it becomes the exchange of "cutting" sarcasm, and "crushing" retort, and "piercing" taunt, &c.

The last stage is Wrath and Rage and Hate proper, and open war and frantic endeavour to suppress each other entirely, physically and mentally, by whatever means and weapons come to hand first, when even Bhíshma and Arjuna, the ideal warriors of the Mahábhárata story, forget the laws of chivalry, and senators in the legislative halls of nations use their fists and fling ink-pots and blue-books at each other.

ii. Repulsion from a superior where the superiority is slight and not definitely recognisable, the desire for inequalisation by making him inferior, coupled with the consciousness of inability to do so, is Apprehension. The physical manifestation is shrinking.

The next degree, where the superiority of the object of dislike is greater, is Fear and Terror proper; the physical manifestation is "avoidance" and "running away."

The third and culminating stage is that of Horror, where the dislike as well as the superiority of its object are at their greatest, and the physical manifestation corresponding to the consciousness of complete inferiority and powerlessness is, "paralysis of the limbs," "powerlessness even to stir and run away.

iii. Repulsion *plus* the consciousness of the inferiority of the object of Repulsion, the desire for further separation from it by means of further inequalisation, and the consciousness of ability to bring about such further inequalisation, is, when the inferiority of the object of Repulsion is slight, mere Supercilousness, Self-importance. The physical manifestation is "looking down upon," "holding the head high," "toss of the head."

In the next degree it is Scorn, Contempt, the physical manifestation of which is the

The third stage is Disdain, manifested in the "spurning away" of the object, the "relentless crushing" of it, "the treading of it into the dust," "planting the heel on the neck," "reducing to slavery," "breaking the spirit."

CHAPTER V.

CERTAIN POSSIBLE OBJECTIONS.

It seems desirable at this stage to consider certain possible objections in detail.

The facts of outright murder on the one hand, and of uttermost self-sacrifice of life on the other, seem to conflict with the theory of the nature of Love and of Hate propounded here. But the reconciliation is to be found in the consideration that even in these cases—when they are true instances of Love and Hate—there is *in the consciousness* the perpetuation of the relation of Love or of Hate, as the case may be.

This explanation will not appear very satisfactory to those who have not yet seen reason to believe that the individual Self, the Jíva, has any life apart from the *present* physical body. Yet the fact of the *consciousness* of a perpetual, unending relation is verifiable by them too. When a person deliberately and voluntarily undergoes suffering for the well-being of another, even to the extent of giving up his life; when he does so silently, in concealment, and unrecognised; when he is, over and above all this, an atheist, an agnostic, a non-believer in a soul and a future life by the conviction of his intelligence; even under all these circumstances, if his mind were looked into with sufficient scrutiny, there would be found in it, a *desire* for recognition, suppressed by some stronger motive; a consciousness, a sub-consciousness it may be, that his act of self-sacrifice might have a permanent, a lasting, nay, a perpetual value; and a long series of the beneficial results of the act would be present in his consciousness, thereby extending that consciousness actually over all that period, notwithstanding the side-belief that the consciousness would be cut short in a limited time. The truth here is that the side-belief is a mere word-belief—there is no real modification of consciousness corresponding to it; consciousness *can never imagine* its own cessation.

मासाब्दयुगकल्पेषु गतागम्येष्वनेकधा ।
नोदेति नास्तमेत्येका संविदेषा स्वयंप्रभा ॥

(Panchadashi I. 7.)

"Through the numberless months, years, yugas and kalpas, past and to come in the exhaustless future, what rises not nor sets is this one Self-luminous consciousness alone."

संविदो व्यभिचारश्च नानुभूतो ऽस्ति कर्हिचित् ॥ १५ ॥
यदि तस्याप्यनुभवस्तर्ह्ययं येन साक्षिणा ।
अनुभूतः स एवात्र शिष्टः संविद्वपुः स्वयम् ॥ १६ ॥

(Devi-Bhágavatam III. 32. xv., xvi.)

"Never has the cessation of consciousness been witnessed; or if it has been, then the witness thereof himself remains as the embodiment of consciousness."

It has just been said that cases of murder and of self-sacrifice of life—when they are true instances of Love and Hate—are reconcileable with the theory put forward here. Other cases do not need such reconciliation and they are no less frequent.

Let us consider what would be true instances of the relinquishment of one's own life and the taking of another for pure Love and pure Hate respectively. And first the precise significance of Love and Hate should be fixed in this reference. Which one or more of the three principal phases of each can be meant here?

On the side of Love, such absolute self-surrender involving complete self-extinction would, at first sight, appear to be possible in the case of all the three phases. A greater might conceivably give himself away wholly to a smaller to enlarge the latter's life. So a smaller might also give himself to the greater and be absorbed into his larger life?] But is this possible? Apparently not, from what has been said before as to the nature of Devotion. The superior cannot take from the lesser, and so increase inferiority. Such an absorption is not possible in the case of equals either. It involves a reasoning in a circle. Each cannot become absorbed in the other, only one may in another. The result is that only a greater can give himself away to a lesser; and the meaning of Love in this special connection is therefore Benevolence.

What is the case on the side of Hate? Equals as equals, and while continuing equals, cannot harm each other. And the lesser can clearly not suppress the greater. Thus in the case of Hate too, only the greater can suppress and take the life of the lesser; and so in this reference Hate means Pride.

Unfortunately the word Pride does not express all that is meant to be expressed. And there does not appear to be another English word—scarcely even a Saṁskrit word, though मदः, *mada*, comes very near to it—to express the exact opposite of Benevolence, to express Hate *plus* superiority in strength *plus* active exercise of both. Tyranny approaches most nearly. Hate, Tyranny, and Pride will therefore be used rather unprecisely in the succeeding paragraphs as each seems fittest and most expressive.

It should also be noted that the words "greater" and "lesser" have been used above in a precise and limited signification, restricted to the ability to give or take life.

Passing on after this preliminary limitation of the signification of Love and Hate in instances of self-sacrifice and of slaughter proceeding from them, we find that the cases where the death, and the death alone, of the physical body of the benefactor is absolutely necessary for the purpose of the benefaction, and is consciously, deliberately, and fully premeditated, are, fortunately for humanity, few. The Buddha, in a previous incarnation, giving up his Bráhmana-body in invincible and joyous tenderness to feed the life of the famishing tigress and her cubs, wives sucking the poisoned wounds of husbands and dying; shipwrecked sailors tossed on rafts for week after week, and casting lots to decide whose body should first be sacrificed to feed his starving comrades; healthy persons giving blood in large quantities for transfusion into the veins of the sick—are very infrequent instances in tradition and history. In most other cases the self-sacrifice of life is incidental and not premeditated, not even strongly expected as probable, as in rescues from fire or water or weapons. In such cases the giving up of life is not necessary, very often the exact opposite is necessary, to the achievement of the object of the action.

In the case of Hate—Pride *plus* Tyranny—unfortunately for humankind, the action whereof the suppression of another's life is the direct and premeditated object is very frequent at this point of small progress in human evolution.

The causes and beginnings of Hate are, in strict theory, not more numerous than those of Love amongst embodied Jívas. But the instinct of Love is unity; hence Benevolence begins by giving up one after another the many things that make up embodied life, in order to secure, in the *receding end*, the unity of two Selves. An utter self-sacrifice of life is therefore seldom required. The instinct of Hate on the other hand is separateness; and where it is strong and rampant it *would begin* by at once taking away—in imagination only if it cannot in actuality—the separate life and Self of the other, as the very root, in order wholly, easily, and effectually to suppress all the rest that constitues the existence of that other. In lawless and savage races the slaughter of human beings, on the slightest occasions, is in consequence immense. But in ordered and well-governed societies—where the very fact of social organisation shows that the elements of Love and harmony and union are more or less prevalent over the elements of Hate and discord and disorder—the Hate is less strong, and would not, or is not allowed to, begin with murder, but generally commences with inflicting minor injuries and losses.

In the result, the fact remains that there is much more murder caused by true Hate than self-sacrifice of life by Love.

Cases of murder for robbery and for sex-jealousy—wherein the "separate Self" seeks its own comfort and preservation and propagation either in and through its own physical body, or in and through its progeny—are cases of rather indirect Hate. There is the desire to gain something which is likely to cause pleasure and enhance life. But as this is a desire in and for the "separate Self," and not in and for the "united Self," there is a conflict over it between the two separate Selves concerned, instead of union; and this conflict becomes the conflict of *manifest* Hate. If there were no such conflict, the underlying Hate would not come to the surface. Cannibals, travellers' accounts say, treat their future victims with great care and tenderness, and fatten them up; and there is no sign of Hate at all in their relations. But let the victim resist his immolation, and Wrath and Hate are at once aroused.

This belongs to travellers' stories, which cannot be verified by everybody's personal experience. Let us take what is within the reach of every one.

Poulterers, and beef, mutton, and pork-breeders feed and tend their animals very carefully, even affectionately—shall we say?—and enhance their life for the time being by fattening them up, and so do exactly what Love would do rather than Hate in similar circumstances. But imagine what the case would be if one of these animals resisted yielding up its flesh when it was required of him to add to the flesh of its master. The rage and roar of wild animals tearing their prey are only due to the resistance of the prey, to its endeavour to keep its flesh for itself. This conflict of desires brings out the hidden Hate. So far as the mere flesh is concerned the tiger loves not its mate more dearly than it loves the antelope. It rends not its mate as it rends the antelope, because it finds in that mate possibilities of repeated pleasures, which can be secured by the fostering of that mate and would be lost by the rending of it. It has no such inducement to preserve rather than destroy in the case of the deer.

In other words, the emphasising of the "united Self" with reference to a common object of desire is Love; the emphasising of the "separate Selves" with reference to a common object of desire is Hate.

In other cases the Hate is more direct. In the case of insults and affronts, of reflections upon each other's superiority, of non-admission of such, of the desire to "cut down tall poppies," &c., &c., the desire to suppress each other has no other distant and indirect motive and object.

प्रकृतिः खलु सा महीयसां सहते नान्य समुन्नतिं यया ॥

(Kirâtâr juniya.)

"It is the very nature of the great and proud that they cannot endure the rise of others." These it may perhaps be said are instances of true Hate causing murder in a special sense.

The deaths in wars are, it may be noted, connected with both Benevolence and Tyranny. In so far as the fighters fight for what they believe to be a righteous cause, and risk their lives for the sake of the general good of their country, they are dominated by the one Emotion; in so far as they fight for mere robbery of land, or money, or similar physical advantages of commerce, &c.—however specious the names given to the causes of the war—they are dominated by the other.

All these cases will, it seems, be covered by the theory of a perpetuation of the relation in consciousness — and so in subsequent lives, according to the Indian doctrine on the subject.

Beginning with Anger, each party to a relation of Repulsion endeavours to separate the other as much as possible from himself. This he seeks to secure by *taking away* from that other all that makes up his being, and so making him inferior to and distant from himself. The other reciprocates and so "exchange of blows" goes on, till the relation of Anger is changed into the relation of Pride on the one hand and Fear on the other. The former then exclaims: "I have broken this creature's spirit." The other bears away in his heart the bitterness and ashes of despair, the ever-burning fire of secret rage, and rankling sense of mortification and malice. This is the commonest development of relations of Repulsion. Sometimes, only too frequently, the relation apparently ends in the death of one party caused by the violence of the other. But so long as the Hate continues in the heart of the survivor, the other party is also present in his mind and to his consciousness, and the relation has not really ended; witness the boasting over destroyed enemies, arches and monuments of triumph, and periodical celebrations, &c., &c. Even when the Hate dies, and is succeeded (through natural reaction coming sooner or later, as it must, in the same life or in another) by Remorse and other subsequent moods, then too the relation between the two continues, the two are still together in consciousness; but the nature of the relation has of course changed.

And so all the component parts, all the Jívas, of a world are and continue to be bound to each other in relations of Love or Hate by the bonds of memory and consciousness, till the bonds are loosened by knowledge in the way that will appear later on.

CHAPTER VI.

THE CORRESPONDENCE OF THE EMOTIONS WITH VIRTUES AND VICES.

From what has gone before it immediately follows that the virtues and vices of mankind are only the Emotions become permanent: they are only permanent moods of feeling, guiding modes of action. In the case of virtues they are the Emotions on the side of Love; in the case of vices those on the side of Hate. Indeed, this is so much the case that, even without the fact being clearly recognised, the same word is often found denoting a particular Emotion as well as the virtue or vice corresponding to it; for instance, compassion and pride. It requires only to name the corresponding Emotions and the virtues and vices side by side respectively to show at once the truth of the statement made above.

The permanent aspects of the principal Emotions named before, appearing in man as overruling and predominant moods of feeling, affecting, colouring, and guiding his modes of action, are:—

On the side of Love:

The Attraction between equals in the three ascending stages before mentioned (pp. 40-42) gives rise to:

Politeness—Good manners—Courtesy—Blandness.

Friendliness—Helpfulness—Sociability.

Lovingness—An affectionate nature—Domesticity.

Attraction to a superior similarly produces:

Modesty—Unobtrusiveness—Mildness.

Reverence — Seriousness — Earnestness — Gravity—Sedateness—Staidness—Non-flippantness.

Meekness—Humility—Obedience—Gratitude.

Attraction to an inferior:

Kindliness — Appreciativeness — Goodwill — Urbanity—Condescension—Suavity.

Gentleness — Softness — Sweetness — Kindheartedness.

Compassionateness — Pitifulness — Benevoence.

On the side of Hate, they are, similarly:

Towards equals:

Rudeness—Brusqueness—Churlishness.

Moroseness — Sullenness — Irascibility — Peevishness.

Cholericness—Bearishness—Ill-temper.

Towards superiors:

Timidity—Suspiciousness—Shyness.

Timorousness.

Cowardice—Vindictiveness—Revengefulness.

Towards inferiors:

Superciliousness — Nil admirari — Slightingness—Self-complacence.

Self-importance—Aggressiveness—Obtrusiveness.

Scornfulness — Disdainfulness — Hauteur—Pride.

The above general list is sufficient illustration of the proposition stated at the beginning of this chapter, and also of the complexity and subtlety of shade which prevails among human Emotions at the present stage of evolution, making indistinguishable the line at which Emotions pass into permanent moods, and become mental facts which are not allowed the name of Emotions in ordinary language, nor even of virtues or vices, sometimes.

This subject leads on immediately to the consideration of a number of mental phases which require careful analysis in order that they may be brought into line with the procession of thoughts followed hitherto.

The complete significance, in all their mental associations, of the facts that are denoted by the words virtue and vice; why the one should be followed and the other eschewed; and many related questions; these belong to the Metaphysic of Ethics, the necessary sequel to the Metaphysic of the Emotions, as the Metaphysic of the Self is its necessary precursor.

The outlines thereof may have to be touched on afterwards in connection with the question (which belongs to a later stage) of the practical cultivation of virtues and the eradication of vices by means of the regulation of the Emotions.

CHAPTER VII.

COMPLEX EMOTIONS.

Many Emotions, virtues, and vices which are pre-eminently called by those names nowadays, and are more prominently noticeable in human intercourse than some of the others before-mentioned, have as yet not even been named amongst those others. The reason for this is that on analysis they appear to be compound rather than simple, made up of more than one of those described before, sometimes of Emotions on the same side, *i.e.* of Love only, or of Hate only, and sometimes of elements taken from both sides. The last kind, indeed, figure the most prominently in present human life, for the reason that they—because of their very nature—involve the greatest and completest exercise and excitement of the whole of human nature, of both sides of it, the good and the bad. The battle between these is sharpest at the turning point in evolution, just before the one is definitely worsted and begins to give way steadily to the other. For this reason these emotions fix the attention and impress the memory in an overpowering degree.

Majesty, dignity, self-control, self-possession, awesomeness, awe, sublimity, grandeur, magnificence, magnanimity, admiration, wonder, pathos, laughter, heroism, devotion, valour, courage, fortitude, endurance, prudence, discretion, cautiousness, circumspection, confidence, trust, faith, diffidence, shyness, distrust, jealousy, envy, ridicule, humour, malice, spitefulness, meanness, niggardliness, criticalness, fault-finding, slanderousness, insolence, crookedness, cruelty, tyranny, impertinence, greed, lust, disgust, disgustingness, loathing, abhorrence, &c., &c. these are instances of complex emotions.

It would appear indeed at first sight that all, or almost all the irreducible Emotions, which had remained behind as hopeless and impossible to classify after the enumeration of those set forth in order previously, had been thrown together pell mell in this list. It is not so. Scrutiny will disclose that the same basic principle of analysis and classification applies to these, and it would be an interesting and instructive lesson for a student to sort out these and the many others not named, and assign to each its proper place in a genealogical scheme of the Emotions.

A brief and rapid analysis of the more important of these will accordingly be attempted here, sufficient to indicate how out of the same simple and homogeneous elements exceeding heterogeneity grows forth.

Let us begin with Majesty, with which the above list commences.

With reference to the fact that current language scarcely tolerates the denomination of Majesty as an Emotion, it may be restated here—it has already been said before in different language—that each Emotion has two aspects, a subjective and an objective. The former is the aspect of the Emotion as felt by the person under its influence, actively feeling it and possessed by it; the latter is that presented to other persons. The Emotions in which the former aspect predominates are the Emotions recognised by ordinary language. Those in which the latter predominates are called merely qualities. These qualities again, if their beneficent or maleficent results to others are prominent, are called virtues and vices respectively. Thus the distinction is only one of relative permanence, as already stated in the chapter on virtues and vices. It is matter of common observation that passing feelings leave almost no trace behind. Great Emotions, long continued, stamp themselves on the features, passing from the predominantly subjective to the predominantly objective phase.

In this sense, there is an Emotion of Majesty underlying and making possible the quality of Majesty—that is, there are present the subjective and objective aspects. And that Emotion is an equal compound of Compassion and Pride—Compassion for the weak, the poor, the good and the deserving; and Pride and repressive strength for the proud and strong and evil and lawless. Such is the virtue that befits the Jívas whose part in life is the part of kings and rulers. And the instinct of man has devised as physical emblem of this, the sceptre or sword of punishment in the one hand of the king, and the globe or bowl or निधिपद्मम् *ṇidhi-padmam*, treasure-lotus of gifts in the other.

Dignity is only a lesser degree of Majesty.

Self-control, Self-possession, Self-respect—these are the beginnings and the foundations of Majesty and Dignity. They stand at the turning-point between the two opposite sets of Emotions. They mean, in their true inner and fullest significance the desire to unite *rather* than to separate, the desire to avoid, *if possible*, the relations of Hate and discord, and to preserve and promote those of harmony and Love. This is their inner, subjective aspect. The outer and objective aspect is "unmovedness," "inaccessibility to emotion," "unemotionalness," "unemotiveness." These words, taking account of only the outer condition of the physique accompanying the inner mental mood, do not describe the actual state of things quite correctly. In fact they are even misleading. They convey the impression that there is no Emotion at all beneath Self-control. The reverse is the fact, especially in the case of Jívas just beginning to acquire the experience, the faculty, the possibility of the Emotion or mood of Self-control and Self-possession. In them the struggle between the opposing desires, the one tending to break out in a violent expression of one or other Emotion on the side of vice, and the other to prevent such an outbreak and cause rather an expression of an Emotion on the side of virtue—this struggle is very strong. It is only gradually that the one nature gains such complete mastery over the other that the struggle, which does continue to take place for long, becomes more and more feeble and unfelt.

The result in the outer man is all through a deadlock, a stillness, an unmovedness. Held back by the strong reins of reason—of Love, which is the highest reason, for it founds on and is that Truth of truths, the unity of Jívas—the wild unbroken horses of the man's lower nature stand in apparent motionlessness. But look not at that outer motionlessness; look rather at the great strain within, if you would understand the true Emotion-nature of Self-control.

The above analysis of Self-control is supported by the ordinary usage of the word. When a person is praised for his Self-control, what is praised in him is his ability to refrain from the expression of one of those Emotions which have been classed above on the side of vice. But sometimes Self-control is used to denote the power of restraining an Emotion on the other side also. This use is due, in the first place, to the confining of the attention to the outer result of the Self-control, in which outer result there is the absence of the appearance of all Emotion, and not only of evil Emotion. In the second place, when the word is used in this second sense, with a laudatory implication, that is due to the special constitution of the races of men amongst whom such use occurs. In them the use is due to the mental mood which has been referred to above, in the analysis of Reserve and Chilliness, in the case of the majority. And in the case of the minority, who *would* express their better Emotions unreservedly, as of Pity by tears, if placed in different circumstances, Self-control, in this sense, occurs either deliberately and intentionally because they see that the demonstration of their Emotion would arouse an evil Emotion—of Scorn or Ridicule or the like—in others; or it occurs unconsciously by force of surroundings and conventions and circumstances, though the real reason may be and is the same.

Heroism is only active Majesty: Majesty as appearing in the moment of action, when the element of Compassion for and helping of the weak, and repression of the oppressor, become manifest in actuality from having been potential. The former element is, if possible, even more prominent than the latter. The very essence of Heroism is giving—the giving of one's property, one's life, one's most cherished possessions, for the succour of a weaker and a younger. Compare the Sanskrit expressions, दानवीरः, दयावीरः, *Dána-vírah*, *Dayá-vírah*, the heroic giver, the hero of Compassion. Public instinct too does not give the epithet of hero to any one, however great his deeds, in whose deeds the fact or possibility of self-sacrifice has not been present, who has not undergone actual suffering or the risk of suffering. In the *Mahábhárata*, Bhíshma, reading the roll of heroes to Duryodhana, denies that title to Droṇa's son, Ashvatthámá, in every way equal to Arjuna himself as warrior, *because* "Ashvatthámá loves his life, and fights not regardless of it."

Courage, Valour, Bravery, Fortitude, Endurance—these are grades and kinds of Heroism; kinds distinguished from each other by the differing circumstances in which the superiority which makes Compassion for the weak and repression of the strong possible, is displayed; and grades distinguished from each other by the varying extents of that superiority.

That Heroism and Courage, &c., should have come to be associated almost exclusively with wars and battles and martial prowess is due to the "accident" that, in the present stage of human evolution, the essential characteristics of these Emotion-virtues are called forth and appear mainly on the occasions of such struggles. But with different social and national circumstances the Heroism and Courage of quiet, unostentatious even unknown, Self-sacrifice in ordinary life, apart from slaughter and massacre, will be recognised more and more prominently, as they have always been recognised, even if not prominently, in all true literature.

Diffidence is the opposite of Shyness. As the latter is incipient fear, is Repulsion *plus* the consciousness of *the possible*, but not certain superiority of the object of the Repulsion, so is Diffidence incipient affection, Attraction *plus* the consciousness of the possible, but not certain, superiority of the object thereof. The outward manifestation of Diffidence is hesitation as to the *manner* of approach, on terms of equality or of inferiority. In the case of Shyness the outward manifestation is hesitation as to approaching at all.

Because of the incipience of both the Emotions it often happens that the words respectively denoting them are used indiscriminately. But compare the usage in such cases as these: "A horse shies at an object that frightens him;" and "Youth and maiden approach each other diffidently."

Where the two are really indistinguishable the proper explanation would probably be that the Emotion is a compound of "*uncertain* desire and *uncertain* consciousness." There is no clear memory of a past contact and of resultant pleasure or pain, and consequently no clear expectation; hence no certain desire either for approach or avoidance, but an oscillation backwards and forwards.

The converse of Diffidence is Confidence, as that of Shyness is Distrust, settled Disbelief. This is plain even in the ordinary usage of words. Confidence in another means Attraction *plus* the consciousness of the certain Benevolence, or Friendliness, or Humility—any one of the three—towards oneself, of the person liked, with reference to another object of desire. This is an illustration of a combination of a simple Emotion in one person with a complex consciousness of an Emotion-virtue in another to form a new Emotion.

Distrust is similarly Replusion *plus* consciousness of the certain Scorn or Anger or Fear towards one Self of the other who is the object of that Repulsion, with reference to another object of desire.

In another view Confidence is the feeling, the consciousness, the certainty of one's own equality to the task, to the occasion, *plus* the desire to approach it and take it up. Lay the stress here on equality and not on task or occasion. Confidence is the feeling—and the feeling may be one either of Attraction or Repulsion —*plus* the consciousness of ability to carry out into action the particular specialised form of that desire, whether one of Attraction or Repulsion. The feeling mostly takes shape as a general excitement or elation, that being the appearance of superiority or ability desirous of, or on the point of, asserting and proving itself. The mere intellectual cognition of one's own power would be only *knowledge*, and not the *Emotion* or *feeling* of confidence, which always hides a desire internally, however calm and unmoved the exterior may be.

The analysis of Distrust under this other view is exactly similar.

Faith, Belief, and Trust, Doubt, Suspicion, and Misgiving, are respectively allied to Confidence and Distrust, and are even sometimes only synonyms of these Emotions.

Devotion has already been alluded to as distinct from Worship. At first sight—inasmuch as it generally and prominently makes a tie between an inferior and a superior—it may indeed appear to be a simple, and not a complex, Emotion of the nature of Worship. But it is in reality complex. Devotion is a Self-surrender, a Self-sacrifice, a giving of all one has to another. Such *giving* necessarily implies superiority in the giver. The inferior receives. But surely if, as already said, the feeling of Devotion is the feeling of an inferior towards a superior, and at the same time Devotion implies giving, and giving implies the superiority of the giver—is there not here an insuperable contradiction in terms?

Let us look closer. It is only *generally*, and not invariably, according to even current language, that Devotion is the feeling of an inferior to a superior. A husband is devoted to his wife, a mother to her infant, a benevolent physician to his patients in a hospital. Is the word "devoted" here misused and misapplied? or are the mother, the husband, the physician, inferior to the objects of their Devotion?

Neither is evidently the case. But a servant is also devoted to his master; a soldier in the ranks to his officer; a disciple to his teacher; a worshipper, a creature, to his Deity and Creator. Here the inferiority is obviously on the side of the devoted person, and the word devoted is equally correctly used.

Is the word then used in two different senses in the two connections? It would appear so. The significance of the word is service and help in both places. What then is the difference? It is this. In the first case the service and help are truly service and help directly to the object itself of the Devotion; and the Devotion here is in reality only Tenderness. That the Tenderness should receive the name of Devotion in this reference is due to the fact that attention has been excessively fixed on the large element of Self-sacrifice in the Tenderness, and on the aspect of persistence which the Tenderness has put on, and which persistence it has in common with the mood which is more appropriately indicated by the word under discussion.

In the second case the persistent service that is implied is *co-service* with the object of devotional attachment to another object altogether. A Deity, a teacher, a superior officer, as such, does not require any sacrifice for himself from his devotee, or disciple, or subordinate. He requires it for others whom he himself is serving and helping: a world, a race, a government, and their respective constituents. *To these*, both the object and the subject of the Devotion are superior, though in vastly different degrees.

So far as the Deity, or teacher, and other superior accept a service to themselves from the inferior, they do so either by giving permission to the inferior to make repayment in his small way of kindness done to him formerly, and thereby to that extent lift him from inferiority to equality, as before said: or they graciously and voluntarily contract a new debt, an obligation to that inferior, to be necessarily repaid in the future, and thereby voluntarily put themselves in the position of the debtor, an inferior to that extent and in that reference; they would probably do so for the educing in the devotee of higher qualities, possible only in connection with a sense of power and confidence. To sum up, Devotion in the sense of Devotion to an ideal, a teacher, a Deity, is Reverence, wherein a partnership in serving others is sought, and however generally inferior the dévotee may be, the very fact of partnership gives a limited equality. Defined in terms of desire, Devotion is the desire for equalisation with the Ideal who is the object of that

Devotion, not merely by direct receipt of gift through prayer, as is the case in pure Worship, but by means of obedience to the behests of and guidance received from that Ideal.

To have to use the words inferior and superior and equal in such connections looks awkward, no doubt, because of the long-established emotional associations of these words. But it is hoped that in the present psychological analysis of Emotions, only the strictly and rigorously scientific significance of the words will be looked at, and all other ordinary associations discarded for the time being. Without such temporary balancing of the mind a useful discussion of the subject will remain impossible.

Loyalty and Fidelity are grades of Devotion. The element of desire, the desire of co-operation, co-service, is less active, less urgent, here; it waits for an occasion instead of seeking one, or even seeking to create one, as Devotion in its excess of zeal sometimes does.

Awesomeness is that aspect of Majesty which deals with the repression of evil, taken by itself; as Benignity is the converse. Awe is the Emotion in the beholder corresponding to the virtue or quality of Awesomeness in the object of that Emotion. The root of the Emotion of Awe is on the side of Hate—Repulsion. It is akin to the Emotion of Fear. A person struck with Awe is a person who realises for the time being the possibility of the existence in himself of deficiencies which would call forth the repressive powers of the object of Awe. He that has no dross in him feels not Awe in the presence of the Highest, but only Worship, Devotion, Love. He that is the Highest purifies not dross by chastisement, but transmutes it by His own overpowering Love into the purity of Love and Devotion, in all that happen to stand in His Presence: He has transcended Majesty and rests in Benignity. Encouragement corresponds to Benignity, as Awe to Awesomeness.

Magnanimity is the Emotion-virtue which is next higher in order after Self-control. Pain caused by another, wrong done by another, no longer arouse struggle; they are simply passed over, absorbed, overlooked. Large-heartedness, Forgivingness, Generosity are practically other names for the same thing. But they have not yet reached the height of perfect Compassion, constant Benevolence.

Unforgivingness, Rancourousness, Vindictiveness, are the counterparts of these on the side of Repulsion.

Strictness, Justice, Implacability, Rigorousness, would be the mean between these two. Honour, Uprightness, Prudence, Discretion, Cautiousness, Circumspection, are all related Emotion-virtues. They all belong to the region of Self-control. In the first the attention is more taken up with "giving others their due"; in the last with "not losing and giving away to others what is not their due."

Jealousy is a peculiar and most powerful Emotion. It seems to be Repulsion *plus* the consciousness of a possible or even probable special kind of superiority in the object thereof, which superiority will enable that person to exclusively gain and appropriate for himself something which is loved, coveted, desired by both. It implies Love of a certain object, and Hate of another person who prevents the exclusive acquisition of that object. In its intenser forms, connected with sex-love, where the Love, the desire for acquisition here, is greatest, the Hate is also naturally at its worst; the consequence is that Jealousy is an Emotion which may be said to disturb the mind of the human being, sway it, tear it in two, more powerfully than any other Emotion. It excites the whole of his dual nature simultaneously in a manner that no other Emotion does.

The Love implied in Jealousy is of course a selfish Love. In Love, as such, there is no selfishness or unselfishness, as said before. It seeks union, which means the equality of both the factors to be united. So long then as the desire for union exists in both the factors of the relation, Love proper is neither selfish nor unselfish—*as between those two.* When, however, the desire for union is only on one side, not on the other, then the desire for union becomes a desire for acquisition, a selfish desire. In Jealousy, the Love, the desire for union, has implicitly become a desire for acquisition, for if, indeed, there were Love on both sides, there would be no chance for intervention by a third party, and Jealousy would not exist in the mind of him that loves and is loved. Also, in whom there is no Exclusiveness, no Reserve, whose gaze of Love is turned not out towards material separateness, but in towards spiritual unity, in him there is no Jealousy.

This leads on to the connected emotion of Lust. The kind of Love that is mostly responsible for the feeling of Jealousy is that which is best denominated Lust. To refined natures it would probably at first sight look impermissible and improper to call Lust a kind of Love at all. Yet there is something in common between them. Later and evil associations, and natural and inevitable consequences, have made the present connotation of Lust a truly evil one. That it was not so always is apparent in the use of the expression "Lusty Youth," where only physical vigour and capacity for physical Love are meant without any depreciatory significance.

As Love in the abstract is desire for union by exchange and equalisation, so Lust is desire for union by exchange and equalisation in the physical self only.

As marriage-unions based on Lust only lead invariably to exhaustion and satiety of the physical nature in a more or less short time, and, the higher mental and spiritual selves not having been cultivated, the higher forms of Love lasting through vast eons of time remain impossible, unhappiness is the logical consequence of such marriage unions, and far more of unions which are not sanctified by even the formalities of marriage—formalities which have at least a shadow of religion and spirituality about them.

It then appears that the evil consequences of Lust, its resultant satiety, exhaustion, weariness, dreariness, and unhappiness, make it evil; otherwise it were not evil; otherwise its consanguinity to Love proper were undisputed. It is the same with other moods of mind to which the word Love is even less hesitatingly applied by mankind. We read that Roman and other epicures "loved" the cooked tongues and brains of nightingales and other delicate birds. The present constitution of the majority of the human race is such that it gladly sanctions the use of the word Love in this connection, and entirely fails to see the horror of the wholesale murder involved. In the strict and abstract sense of the word, however, even this use is perfectly correct; it is only the "consequences" involved that throw this gloom over the word in this reference. As Bhíshma said:

नहि मांसं तृणाद्‌ काष्ठादुपलाद्वापि जायते ।
हत्वा जंतुं ततो मांसं तस्माद्दोषस्तु भक्षणे ॥

"Flesh groweth not on grasses, nor on trees, nor on stones: Flesh is obtained only by killing a living creature; hence only the sin of eating it."

It may be noted here that the more Love is confined to the physical self, the more it is Lust; the more it approximates to an "appetite," a sense-craving, the less it has of the character of Emotion proper.

The so-called mystery of physical Love may not inappropriately be considered here. The question of course belongs, as usual, to Metaphysic, the Metaphysic of the Jíva in the procreative aspect. But a brief statement may throw light on the question more immediately dealt with here.

Amongst the primary so-called lowest organisms, procreation, self-multiplication, is asexual. A cell absorbs nourishment and grows; it expands itself at the expense of something else, another self (in the general sense). Its own oneness grows. But the mass of matter that makes up its "oneness," its "individuality," carries within itself the principle of manyness inherently. It therefore necessarily, inevitably, falls apart into two sooner or later. But in falling apart, the new, the second mass retains the nature of "livingness" it has acquired during the period of oneness; and so becomes the centre of the new life of an individual similarly constituted; another Jíva of the same class at once comes in and occupies the ready-made, specially-prepared home. Trace the process up from **उद्भिज्जः** *udbhijjah*, born by fission, separation, or sprouting, through **स्वेदजः** *svédajah*, sweat-born, by exudation, and **अण्डजः** *Aṇḍajah*, egg-born, into **पिंडजः** *pindajah*, sexual humanity, step by step. The kind, the essential nature, of the process is exactly the same in essence, but the manner has changed completely. The "expansion" of one embodied Jíva, which was in the first instance caused by direct actual and real nourishment—comparatively speaking, for from the standpoint of the ultimate that is also truly illusory, an atom being always a vortex of movement and resistance in an imaginary some one thing—is now caused by an excitement of the multiple senses and organs of that Jíva by an appropriation of another embodied Jíva, which appropriation is only the simulation and the substitute of the process of the absorption of nourishment.

In the simulation and substitution is the mystery. Each Jíva Upádhi attracts the other in order to absorb it into itself and so enlarge its own life; and at the same time each repulses the other to avoid being absorbed into it. This is mutual. Attraction prevailing largely over Repulsion—the latter becoming reduced to a mere consciousness of separate individual existence in the highest forms of Love—there is mutual approach and a *simulation* of absorption and nourishment, but not complete and real absorption and nourishment. And here appetite and desire pass into the form of Emotion.

The separation into sexes, at a certain stage, the middle one, in Evolution, is Nature's master-device for bringing easily within the reach of each Jíva a compendium of all experiences—though it is, as *compared with* the originals of the experiences, viz., the experiences resulting from the contact of the senses with the aspects of nature, Prakṛiti at large—only a false copy, however overpowering for the time being. And the separation of sexes seems to be brought about by the easy means—though requiring ages and eons to mature—of a separation of functions, of producing after taking, and of giving and then guarding, the paternal and the maternal, both brooded over by the Love which here is the retention of "oneness" even after the "falling apart," and is the foundation of the Family, the Tribe, the Nation, and the Race. This division into sex is itself a copy of that primal and essential division into Self and Not-Self; and as that division is the necessary condition of all experience, so is sex-division nature's cheapest, easiest, and most successful way of giving to every one of her Jívas experience of the noblest and the vilest, the intensest and the dullest, Sensations and Emotions. Truly are man and woman the whole of the world unto each other while this sex-separation lasts.

Where again this physical Love, this Lust, is entirely one-sided, there result the Emotion and action of Rape, which excites not only the physical self, but also the Emotions of Pride and Oppression. These, in the evil of the two classes, good and evil, of Jívas, become pleasureable by being accompanied with a sense of power and superiority, as will appear later.

The commonness of Adultery, too, in a great deal of modern life is due to similar reasons. Adultery excites not only the emotion of Lust, but of Malice, sometimes of Revenge, or of Pride and Conquest, and again of Fear which—by a particular perversion that will be treated later on in more detail under the subject of the Philosophy of Poetry and Literature—becomes in a certain aspect a pleasurable, from being an originally painful, sentiment.

The real and full significance of the statement in the *Bhagavad-Gítá*, संकरो नरकायैव "Adultery leadeth into hell," is to be found in this very fact that it has its root in the evil Emotions, and so shall have branches and fruits in them too. If the springs of the stream are poisoned, all its subsequent length will show the taint. Let the Emotion, the whole mood of the parents, be pure, peaceful, happy, and loving in the moment they produce and "set apart" from their own Upádhis a new Upádhi, and then this nucleus, partaking as it must of the pure nature of its parent Upádhis, shall become fit abode for a pure Jíva. Otherwise it will be evil and attract an evil Jíva only into itself. Herein is to be found the true use and significance of a formal and public celebration and consecration of marriage, whereby all false and evil Emotions of Shame and Fear of other claimants are removed, and only pure and peaceful and undisturbed affection is given the best opportunity of growing between the married pair, to the benefit of the progeny.

The converse of Jealousy—viz., Attraction

plus the consciousness of a possible superiority in another which will *help* one to secure the object of one's wish — has apparently no distinctive name in the English language. Confidence, Trust, Faith, are the nearest terms. Perhaps the idea is better expressed by Hopefulness; the Emotion in the parent corresponding to the Hopefulness, the Promisingness, of his child; the Emotion which is indicated in the Saṁskrit saying:

सर्वत्र जयमन्विच्छेत् पुत्रादिच्छेत् पराजयम् ॥

"Let a man wish to excel all others, but let him wish that his son should excel him."

Envy is Jealousy wherein the superiority of the object thereof is more pronounced, the Repulsion as great, and the active endeavour to make the envied person inferior to oneself is weaker, because less hopeful. Jealousy and Envy cease as soon as the disputed object is definitely secured by one of the rivals: the Emotion that is left behind in the mind of the loser is then neither Envy nor Jealousy, but Hate—the Hate of Malice.

Malice is Hate *plus* Fear. Its converse is Tyranny, Cruelty, Oppression. Many that call call others malicious and mean are worse themselves, for they are oppressors and misappropriators, have themselves by their own action created Malice and Meanness in their victims, and are angry that they should be resisted by those victims in the ways that appear malicious and mean. Spitefulness is allied to, perhaps the same as, Malice.

Meanness is Strictness where Benevolence or Magnanimity is expected and proper. Niggardliness is an allied Emotion. Usage confines the word to money matters.

Extravagance, Carelessness, Recklessness, False Magnificence, are the converse moods. They are Benevolence where strictness is desirable.

Insolence, Impertinence, Stiff-neckedness, Stiff-backedness, Brag, Bullying, Presumptuousness, &c., are also all converse moods, in another way. They are the assumption in oneself of equality or superiority where the fact is inferiority to the object of the mood. The desire here is the desire of Repulsion, though it is not very prominent in the beginning. An "insult" is the pointed expression of one's consciousness of the inferiority of the object of the insult.

Crookedness and Craftiness are the more active forms of Spitefulness and Malice; but the element of dislike is more hidden.

Admiration too appears to be a complex Emotion. Of course, in order to say that an Emotion which is described by a special name is simple or complex, we must be guided by current usage in deciding what Emotion is really denoted by that word. This reflection comes up at once in connection with a word like Admiration, which is used — like so many others, on account of the paucity of languages resulting from the absence on the part of the races using those languages of the feeling of any need for more minute and elaborate expression —to indicate many distinguishable though related phases of the same mood. For our present purpose we have to take the sense in which the word is used most often. Taking that sense, *i.e.*, scrutinising the majority of the particular instances in which the word is used, it appears that it is employed mostly where there is a consciousness of the superiority of the object of it, but the feeling of Attraction accompanying it is neutralised or diminished by collateral circumstances.

We admire the skill of a juggler. We recognise the superiority of skill and are pleased with and like the results, but not very much. They appear trivial to us, or perhaps even wasteful of time and energy. So also we admire the skill of a general in the successful conduct of a war. But, if we are neutral to the parties warring, while recognising the superiority of skill in manipulating armies, we are perhaps full of sadness and regret at the fearful results in slaughter and rapine. If we are not neutral but interested, then there is no Admiration: the successful fighter becomes an object of apotheosis or satanisation; his name becomes a name to worship or a name to fear. Again, we admire the beauty of a person; we admit the superiority in that respect, but there is something, some drawback, which prevents the Attraction from ripening into Reverence or Love, and the feeling remains one of Admiration only.

Thus Admiration is Attraction *plus* consciousness of superiority in the object in some respects, *plus* consciousness of its inferiority in some other respects. It comes very near to Esteem. In Esteem the element of Attraction is stronger perhaps, and the objects of it, the attributes liked, are different; they are qualities of a work-a-day usefulness, *indirectly* pleasurable. In the case of Admiration they are more directly pleasurable. Such seems to be the distinction between them; but it refers, of course, to only one special sense and use of each term.

Wonder is distinct from Admiration: yet it has something in common with it too. It is consciousness of the superiority of the object, *plus* attraction, the desire to approach, *plus* uncertainty of one's own ability to do so; the whole being overshadowed by the unexpectedness of the object, it being something out of the ordinary course of experience. It is this extraordinariness, indeed, which is the immediate cause of the uncertainty as to ability to approach. The physical manifestation is a general expansion of the features—open eyes, open mouth, "wide-eyed wonder"—consequent on the feeling of pleasure, accompanied by the arrest of motion—"standing stockstill," "struck dumb"—which corresponds naturally to the uncertainty above-mentioned.

The Emotion stands close to Admiration on the one hand, and Awe and Diffidence on the other: yet there is a subtle distinction between them.

The mystical, the mysterious, the curious—the Emotions of these are allied to the Emotion of the wonderful. There do not seem to be exact names expressing those Emotions, as Wonder describes the Emotion produced by the wonderful. The special, constitutional characters of the objects of the Emotions, and their greater or less extraordinariness and importance, make the difference between them.

Curiosity is "the *desire* for the curious." It is thus a desire for a desire. In strict analysis—as will appear later on—a desire for a desire is an impossibility, and the expression, which has gained currency because it provides a convenient way of expressing some rather common moods of mind, really means (1) directly, a desire for certain pleasurable objects, and (2) indirectly, a desire for a certain condition of oneself, in which condition the fulfilment of the former desire is possible.

Curiosity is an Emotion that afflicts many human beings disproportionately and inappropriately, and very often to the inconvenience of others. What is the meaning of this mood more precisely? When a sick man, who has lost all appetite, desires appetite, *i.e.* desires desire for food, what does he really want? He wants all the pleasurable foods and objects that he enjoyed in his preceding healthy condition, but is prevented from enjoying by his ill-health. Instead of stating the fact at such length, he shortly says he wants his appetite back again. As appetite is to the sick man, as nourishment generally is to the new-born infant, so is "the curious" to the infant individuality and weak soul. Children are full of Curiosity; so are savages. The growing Jíva, not yet full with its own long-gathered experiences, experiences a standing want of more and more, newer and newer experiences, and supplements its own by prying into and vicariously acquiring the experiences of others.

Surprise, Astonishment, &c., are modifications of the Emotion of Wonder. The words are sometimes used to express corresponding moods on the side of Repulsion also by analogy and for convenience.

The Emotion of "the Sublime" is also akin to Wonder. Where the unexpectedness and extraordinariness are at their lowest and the superiority at its highest, the Emotion of "the sublime" is present. Awe is closely related also. The difference is, as is apparent from the foregone analysis of that Emotion, that whereas in that there is a faint degree of Fear here there is only Attraction.

"The wonderful," "the sublime," and "the awful" cluster more frequently, or at least as often, round "inanimate" natural scenes—mountains, summits of snow, gorges, cañyons, lakes, forests, tropical or hill-vegetations, waterfalls, rivers, oceans—than, or as, round human beings — wielders of mystic powers, teachers, doers of great deeds, benefactors of mankind, great writers or great speakers. These scenes and objects of nature are said to arouse these Emotions only by a metaphor, only as invested with human attributes in imagination, which, of course, may be so strong as to stimulate reality. Grandeur and Magnificence are allied to, sometimes synonymous with, Sublimity.

Disgust is Fear in some respects *plus* Scorn in others.

Loathing, Abhorrence, are allied Emotions and express phases of Hate. As to what is the exact phase expressed by each—this is a matter apparently not very easy to determine, as the use of the words does not seem to be very precise or specific. They express Repulsion from an inferior, the cause of the Repulsion being its ugliness *plus* uncleanliness, and imply a desire for physical distance due to a fear of pollution. This latter element is predominant in Loathing, which may even cause the physical manifestation of vomiting, the effort of the body to throw out that which infects or injures it. In Abhorrence the mental element predominates; it is more aggressive than loathing, and may be said to push away the abhorred object, whereas loathing shrinks away from it.

These have an underlying basis of Emotion, because they are not passive but active qualities, and manifest themselves in action, even though it be not always very prominent.

Greed is obviously excess of desire with reference to any particular object. It is then not a complex Emotion.

Tantalisation is a mixture of "the desire to give, to impart," and "the desire to hold back." The reason may be mere Love or Vanity, and Fear of consequences or even Dislike respectively.

The consideration of the Emotion of the Beautiful has been left over to so late a stage, because a peculiar mysteriousness is attached to it by humanity at large, though in reality there appears to be no mystery about it, and though it even appears to be a simple rather than a complex Emotion.

The Emotion of the Beautiful seems to be Love pure and simple: and this is why mysteriousness attaches to it, for it does to Love also. Whatever gives us pleasure, whatever is fit to be united with and added to us, whatever enhances ourself, our life, is, so far, Beautiful to us. The instinct of common usage and language indicates and embodies this truth. The Beautiful is the pleasant, the agreeable, the attractive, the charming, the fascinating, the lovely, the lovable. In Sanskrit—सुंदरम् *sundaram* (सुद्रियते *su driyate*—that which is respected, loved; or सु उनत्ति *su unatti*—that which attracts); रुचिरम् *ruchiram* (रोचते *rochate*—that which shines, or pleases); चारु *chάru* (चरति मनसि *charati manasi*—that which dwells and moves in the mind); सुषमं *sushamam* (सु *su* and समं *samam*—even, unobstructing); साधु *sάdhu* (साध्नोति *sάdh-noti*—fulfils desires); शोभनम् *shobhanam* (shining); कांतं *kάntam* (is loved, desired); मनोरमं *mano ramam* or मनोहरं *mano haram* (pleases or steals and attracts the mind); रुच्यं *ruchyam* or रम्यं *ramyam* (is pleasing); मनोज्ञं *manognyam* (knows or fills the mind); मंजु *manju* (is reputed, well-known, or has a sweet and pleasant sound); मंजुलं *manjulam* (the same as the last).

There is no other standard mark of Beauty; for it varies, so far as its outer embodiment goes, with varying tastes in different men, and different races and different times; but it never varies so far as its inner characteristic of pleasantness is concerned. *That* is most beautiful to any one individual which is best calculated to supplement, to duplicate, to doubly enhance his Self, his life. The instinctive, and not the definite, perception of the possibilities of such enhancement makes the mystery of the Emotion. It may be that in later and more advanced races, with clearer vision and wider knowledge of all the phases of human life in each individual, the mystery will disappear and only the Emotion remain.

Primarily this test of Beauty, in its enhancement of another's life, applies to the physical embodiment; secondarily, at a later stage of evolution, when the inner natures have grown, to the emotional and intellectual constitutions.

Vanity, according to the ordinary use of the word, is something reprehensible. Yet on examination it appears to be an Emotion on the side of Attraction, and so on the side of virtue. Like Curiosity it seems to be a double desire, the desire of the desire for union, the desire of Love, the desire to love and be loved. The physical consequence is self-adornment: otherwise too the laying out of oneself to please, in endless ways. That it has come to acquire an evil association is due to two causes. Even in the above good sense, Vanity would be an object of contempt to Jívas in whose constitution Unlovingness, Hardness, Reserve, and "separateness" generally, were strong. Again, the word is used in a different sense altogether, as the nominal derivative of the adjective vain: then it means Self-complacence, Self-satisfaction, and becomes only a modification of Pride, which is a very different Emotion altogether.

Perhaps the reason why the two so different senses have come to be combined in one and the same word is that attention has been exaggeratedly confined to this aspect of the true Emotion, viz., the consciousness of *the ability* to please (and so far, of a certain power, a superiority), which is always present in Vanity together with the desire to please, though the consciousness may be of an ability varying from the lowest to the highest grades. This consciousness of *ability* is present in Self-complacence also; but there it is not an ability to please at all; and this makes all the difference. Vanity *plus* consciousness of something which takes away from the feeling of ability is Shame.

Self-complacence and Self-satisfaction are Self-importance and Superciliousness, in which the consciousness of the inferiority of another has become vague and general, and attention is mostly confined to the consciousness of one's own superiority generally.

Laughter, as has been generally recognised by psychologists all the world over, is the physical manifestation of a sudden and excessive recognition of one's own superiority. Where this consciousness is accompanied by Repulsion, the laugh becomes the laugh of "ridicule": where the "ridicule" is light-hearted, not serious, only chaff and banter, where it is moreover openly and unmistakably pretended and make-believe, the laugh of "jest" and "joke," of "fun" and "good humour" and "good company" results.

But we very seldom find the laugh combined with genuine, deep-seated, real, earnest Benevolence. The smile is the nearest approach to laughter there.

Smiles and tears require careful examination. Jívas smile for joy and smile sadly; they weep in gladness and they weep in pain. What is the meaning of this?

The "smile of joy" has already been incidentally and very briefly explained in connection with Kindness. The essential, psychological meaning of "the expansion of the features in a smile" is a consciousness of "moreness," of "superiority." The receiver of a gift smiles after the receipt. The giver smiles before the gift. In the first case the recipient becomes "more" than he was before. The giver feels that he is more than the object of his charity and kindness. This last smile, the tender smile of Benevolence is very nearly allied to and always ready to pass into the tears of pity. The "smile of sadness" also expresses the sense of superiority of him who smiles to the cause of his sadness, but without Repulsion, rather with patience, with resignation, with hope of future Love. The "cynical smile," "the smile of bitterness," is of course a near relative of the "laugh of scorn."

"The tears of joy," like the "tears of pity," may mean either only an overflow of the superfluous possessions of the Self—but without a definite object as in the other case, and only as a general expression of goodwill to all and readiness to give to any that need; or they may really be, as they often are, tears of pity for one's own past Self, weak and worthy of pity before the cause of joy made it large and strong.

"The tears of pain" are in reality only "tears of pity" where the object of pity is oneself. The Self here divides itself into two, the one pitying, the other suffering and pitied. Tears of pain are thus tears of Self-pity. Tears generally do not come until the pain becomes mixed with a cognitional, considering, thinking, Self-conscious element. This may be observed in children as well as in grown-up persons. A child generally accompanies his crying with exclamations of "I am hurt," or "I have fallen down," or "So and so has struck me." In adults too there are seldom tears during the actual intensity of a pain. Tennyson's beautiful lyric illustrates the fact.

> Home they brought her warrior dead;
> She nor wept nor uttered cry . . . .
> Rose a nurse of ninety years,
> Placed his child upon her knee,
> Like summer showers came her tears:
> "Sweet, my child, I'll live for thee."

This also give us a clue to the reason why tears and Self-pity, while allowed in the weak and the young, are considered reprehensible and unmanly in the grown-up and the strong. The ability to weep, as such, implies a lowering, an abatement, a diminution, a cessation of real acute pain; and to make a parade of pain then appears improper, in the first place; and, in the second place, such Self-pity implies a demand for help by display of one's needs, and this in certain temperaments arouses Scorn, and calls forth the epithets of "whining" and "moaning," &c.

Self-scorn, Remorse, are similar to Self-pity in respect of the dual character. So, too, Self-praise.

The subject leads on directly to Pathos and "the Pathetic." The "luxury of grief" has puzzled psychologists all the world over. The Saṁskrit authors on Sáhitya, too, give no adequate explanation. Sometimes they even content themselves with saying that the enjoyment of the Emotion requires a special and cultivated sense—which is scarcely true, as the Emotion is appreciated by young and old, cultured and uncultured alike. Herbert Spencer says he finds himself baffled: yet he makes a good attempt and brings out some of the real factors of the explanation. It is enough here to say that the essential constituent of the Emotion of the pathetic is Pity, in some phase or other. As to how it becomes a source of enjoyment, &c., will be treated of in detail later in connection with the Philosophy of Poetry.

Persistent pleasure and pain, transformed into joy and sorrow, persistent gladness and sadness take on the characters of Emotions. They seem to be double desires, like Curiosity and Vanity. Persistent sadness seems to be a dissatisfaction, a constant desire that certain things were otherwise than as they are, so that then pleasure and Love would result naturally in place of the present pain and effort and more or less Repulsion. Gladness is the reverse, a satisfaction, a desire to prolong present conditions.

The active aspects of sadness and gladness are Worry and Cheerfulness. As Worry is an Emotion which is the source of a great deal of trouble to humanity, it might be useful to understand it a little more fully. The following factors of Worry are immediately recognisable—(*a*) A going wrong of something, an obstruction to desire, a source of pain; (*b*) endeavour to set matters right and want of success therein; a failure; (*c*) a non-recognition of the impossibility of setting things right and so avoiding the pain; on the contrary, a persistent consciousness that it is possible; (*d*) consequent repeated endeavour and repeated failure; and lastly (*e*), continued anger and annoyance with the cause of the failure, and the mental repetition, over and over again persistently, of the cause of the trouble and the failure to get rid of it. It is this last which gives its peculiar characteristic to Worry; the irritation is worst, naturally, when the cause of the failure to set things right is the unamenability of some human being on whose co-operation the setting right of things depends. If this element of Anger is taken away, then the element in the peculiar painfulness of Worry disappears. All that remains is rightful and justifiable repetition of endeavour to set things right.

It is time to bring this chapter to a close. The list of Emotions might be prolonged indefinitely. The bulk of every language of an intellectually advanced race, excluding technical names, will be found to consist of words dealing with and expressing some phase or other of an Emotion. It is impossible to deal with all of them in one place. Illustration of the general principles expounded earlier was the purpose of this chapter. It is hoped that this has been achieved by the examples given. The student should find sufficient reason herein to believe that all Emotions are capable of being reduced into terms of Love and Hate permuted and combined with grades and kinds of superiority, equality, and inferiority. And he should try to find justification or refutation of his belief in practical exercise with new phases of Emotion.

CHAPTER VIII.

THE CORRESPONDENCE OF EMOTIONS.

Before passing on to the Philosophy of Poetry and the other Arts wherein Emotions are dealt with in an aspect different from that treated of hitherto, a word may be said as to the correspondence of these mental phenomena with each other and how the presence of one calls another into existence.

The general law governing their reciprocation and mutual manifestation may be summed up shortly: *Emotions tend to create their own likeness*, even as fire does. But in the actual workings of life the results of the law undergo modifications by the special circumstances of the cases. These modifications may be generalised under two rules. (*a*) Amongst ordinary Jívas, inclined strongly neither to the side of Love nor to the side of Hate, Emotions produce their own likeness or counterpart. (*b*) Amongst Jívas belonging definitely to the one class rather than the other, the Emotions of others, whether those Emotions belong to the side of Love or of Hate, create the corresponding Emotions of that class only to which the Jívas belong.

Thus, amongst ordinary people, Love will produce Love, and Anger Anger, assuming equality. Pride and Scorn and oppression will inspire Fear and Malice and Vindictiveness in the really inferior; equal or greater Pride and Scorn and oppression in the really superior and stronger; or merely Anger and Annoyance in the really equal. Again Fear and Distrust will inspire Pride and Scorn in the superior; and equal Fear and Distrust in the really inferior; or mere Anger and Annoyance in the really equal. So Benevolence will inspire Humility or Love or Benevolence. And again, Humility will evoke Benevolence or Love or Humility.

But in a Jíva belonging, say, to the class of Jívas in whom the "united Self" is strong, belonging, that is, to the side of virtue and Love—whether this be the case by deliberate cultivation, such as will be treated of in the final chapter, or otherwise, by birth, karma, &c.—the sight of Fear will not arouse Scorn but Benevolence, equally with the sight of Humility; that of Anger, Sullenness, and Moroseness will not inspire real Annoyance and Reserve and withdrawal, but, on the contrary, effort to break down the other's crust-wall of evil mood, and Love and Affection equally with the sight of Love and Affection; that of Pride will not evoke Fear, but true Humility, and the feeling that the other is really better than himself, even as will the sight of Benevolence. And, conversely, in a Jíva belonging definitely—by voluntary, premeditated development in that direction, or otherwise—to the dark side, the sight of Hate and vice, the sight of Humility, or Fear, will equally provoke Disdain and Scorn and Contempt; that of Love or Anger, Sullenness; and that of Benevolence or Pride, Fear and Distrust.

The correspondence may be worked out and observed through all grades and kinds of Emotion. The details are numberless as humanity.

As to why one Emotion should arouse another Emotion at all, as to why reaction should follow action—this belongs to the province of Metaphysic, and final solutions must be looked for there. But it may perhaps help to make the matter less mysterious-looking if the laws gathered above are put in other words.

Why does a display of Fear arouse Scorn? To show Fear of another person is to imply, to indicate, to say, that that person is not worthy of Trust, that there is a relation of Dislike and Hate between him and the timid person. This again is to imply, and to give cause to the other person to believe, that he should expect resistance, and harm, and "attempt at making him less" at the hands of the person who so displays Fear, for the Dislike present in Fear involves consciousness of pain and loss experienced in the past, and imagination of more to be experienced in the future, and *consequent possibility of an endeavour to retaliate.* The natural consequence is, that he, taking up the relation at this last stage, assumes the corresponding vicious attitude, and calls up Anger and Annoyance to his help, these being the ordinary Jíva's resources for supplying its deficiencies and losses. The other, the *fearing*, takes the situation up anew at this stage. And so, by action and reaction, the evil goes on perpetuating itself and becoming ever stronger, instead of abating.

So Malice is created by oppression and Insolence, and by reaction creates greater Contempt and oppression till the whole situation ends in disaster—witness the mutual relations of Bhíma and Duryodhana in the *Mahábhárata;* witness in our own day the mutual relations of so many conquering and conquered races. Such oppressed persons nurse their grievances, and the Emotion, gathering strength with imprisonment and restraint, often explodes suddenly and, to those who do not follow up its gradual growth, in a manner entirely unaccountable and unintelligibly disproportionate to the occasion. These explosions may range from harmless and ludicrous outbursts up to crimes; from cases where a man really weak, but wishing to appear strong, puts in too much loudness and bravado in his first speech to the disliked person and then fails and collapses altogether, to cases where the disliked person is assassinated for imagined wrongs. Wherever there appears capriciousness, or disproportion, or suddenness of action, there imagination has been at work strengthening the Emotion which bursts forth.

The explanation in the other cases relating to ordinary Jívas is exactly similar.

In the case of extraordinary Jívas this new fact comes into play, viz., that they each look only at the actual superiority, or inferiority, or equality underlying the Emotion of another, and mostly ignore that particular aspect of desire which, together with the superiority, &c., makes it the Emotion that it is; and so looking, they impose on it the Emotion corresponding to their own nature and dictated by their reason as the one proper to assume and act upon for practical purposes.

It may be useful to put the above in the form of a table:—

(*a*) LAW No. I.

The sight, in another, of

	PRIDE.	BENEVOLENCE.	ANGER.	LOVE.	FEAR.	HUMILITY
Will inspire in the *ordinary* Jīva if it is Superior	Pride	Benevolence	Pride	Benevolence	Pride	Benevolence
Equal	Anger	Love	Anger	Love	Anger	Love
Inferior	Fear	Humility	Fear	Humility	Fear	Humility

(*b*) LAW No. II.

The sight, in another, of

		PRIDE *or* BENEVOLENCE.	ANGER *or* LOVE.	FEAR *or* HUMILITY.
Will equally arouse in the definitely *virtuous* Jíva, if he is	Superior	Benevolence	Benevolence	Benevolence
	Equal	Love	Love	Love
	Inferior	Humility	Humility	Humility
And in the definitely *vicious* Jíva, if he is	Superior	Pride	Pride	Pride
	Equal	Anger	Anger	Anger
	Inferior	Fear	Fear	Fear

CHAPTER IX.

EMOTION IN ART.

(*a*) POETRY AND LITERATURE.

The Essential Nature of Poetry and Literature. So far we have dealt with Emotions as *desires*; and desire is their true and essential nature. In order to understand the Philosophy of Poetry and Literature we have to refer back to that view of Emotion wherein it is regarded as a pleasurable or painful state *sui generis.* The paragraph on the pleasurable and painful nature of the Emotions on pp. 27-29, should here be read over again. "The Desire-Emotion specialised by the immediately surrounding circumstances of the particular situation is one thing, and the pleasure or pain specialised by its correspondence with such Desire-Emotion is another thing." The latter, the specialised pleasure, is, it would appear, the true significance of the word रस *rasa*, in Saṁskrit, in the

Science of Poetry. And it is in this sense that what Bain (in his work *On Teaching English*, p. 214) tentatively says is true: "To Emotion we must come at last in any precise definition of poetry."

The last word on the subject was said when it was declared that **वाक्यम् रसात्मकं काव्यं**, "Speech ensouled by rasa is Poetry," by Shauddhodani, Vámana, Vishvanátha, and a host of others, all following the lead of Bharata, the sage who first expounded the Science and Art of Poetry and Drama in India. This word remains final, notwithstanding attempts made here and there, notably by Mammata in his *Kávya Prakásha*, to invent other definitions. These attempts are failures by the general verdict, and even the authors of them find themselves compelled to resort to the ordinary view again and again.

The most important word of this definition is clearly the word *Rasa*. Many have been its interpretations and many its translations. Its ordinary non-technical meaning gives the clue to its true special meaning in the Science of Poetry—as declared by Bharata himself. That meaning is "juice, sap," and also "taste, relish." When an Emotion-desire appears in the mind, and is not allowed to rush out in its usual course into action, but is checked, held in, and circumscribed by the cognitive consciousness, and the pleasurable picture of the fulfilment of the desire is deliberately dwelt upon and leisurely enjoyed in the mind, even as a delicious morsel of food may be detained and slowly and fully tasted in the mouth – then comes into existence this peculiar modification of consciousness which is called *Rasa.* *Rasa* is the pleasurable consciousness, the feeling of specialised pleasure, accompanying the presence in the imagination of the picture of the fulfilment of a desire. Compare the use of the word in the Yoga system of Philosophy in the expression रसास्वाद *Rasásváda*, used to indicate one of the activities of the mind, viz., tasting the sweets of imagination, "building castles in the air," which is an obstacle in the way of gaining समाधि *samádhi*—fixity in the higher consciousness.

In *Rasa* there is an intimate interblending of the cognitive and feeling elements of consciousness, with the result that either gains in surface and expanse, but loses in compactness and depth. It is as if two heaps of two different kinds of grain were shaken into each other. The whole new heap would acquire a new colour different from that of either, and would be also larger in size than either. But the colour would probably be vaguer, dimmer, less distinct and defined, than that of either. The resultant, in other words, gains something and loses something. The same result is noticeable in the case taken above from the gustatory consciousness.

Take another simile—a stream of water rushing onwards. If such a stream were led into a circular basin whence there was no outlet, the stream would turn upon itself and revolve round and round and become a whirlpool, growing ever stronger in its circular rush, and ever deeper, if the inflow continued; or stiller and more equable and steady of depth if it were cut off. In either case a certain depth would be gained greater than that of the flowing stream, and a certain spread of surface would be lost.

The characteristic of Poetry is such *Rasa*. Its business is to call up an Emotion and then hold it in, so that its correspondent feeling of pleasure is "tasted" at leisure.

The limiting, the circumscription, is provided by the patent fact that the story, the description, the occasion, is only an imaginary and not a real and personal one for the reader. He is reading the experiences in a book and not passing through them in actual life. Later on, when the man is able to put himself in the position of the student and reader of life, and can regard his own actual life as a book merely, he can treat this in exactly the same way as the reader of the book of ink and paper treats the story written therein; and then the Emotions aroused by and in such actual life have no greater power over him than those aroused by a book of poetry. But it must be remembered that the study and reading of life is not its own end. It is a means to the improvement of life as end. And, unless this aim is held constantly before the mind, great error will result. We meet with people here and there, and indeed more and more frequently in modern times, who have attained to that degree of Self-consciousness that all their life has become deliberate "acting": but inasmuch as the Self, to the consciousness of which they have attained, is not the "united Self," the supreme Self, the Pratyagátmá, their acting is aimless, purposeless, and in the end becomes very dreary and desolate, and remains such till they learn better.

Where the Emotion aroused by the plain narrative is not sufficiently strong in itself, or the pleasure corresponding to it is of such kind that the author or reader wants it lengthened and continued, the device of "ornaments of speech" is resorted to. The sole business of an ornament, of all ornaments, is to put a circle, a limit, round a special feature, to put a marker on it; to thus direct attention to it and intensify the consciousness thereof; and thereby to define and intensify the special beauty of that feature

—for enhancement of beauty is literally nothing else than enhancement of the consciousness of that beauty.

Such "ornaments of speech," "figures of speech," in literature supply the place of the constant "inflow" referred to above in the illustration taken from flowing water, and they give the further supply that is necessary to make the "whirlpool" deeper and stronger and more lasting. The absence of the supply causes the *Rasa* to lose its force and subside into placidity shortly.

From the above considerations it appears that the main and direct object of Poetry is, as Mammata says correctly in this instance, परनिर्वृति, *Para-nirvriti* — great and peculiar pleasure. The other objects he enumerates, *viz.*, instruction in the ways of the world, knowledge of old customs, counsel as to proper action in special situations, &c.—these are secondary and more in accordance with the views of the school of Purva-Mimánsa as to the purpose of language generally than with the views of poets.

(*b*) THE NATURE OF PLEASURE AND PAIN WITH REFERENCE TO VARIOUS CLASSES OF JÍVAS.

The object and nature of Poetry have been thus generally outlined. The nature of *Rasa*, however, cannot be fully understood unless we enter into detail as to the nature of pleasure and pain from the standpoint of Metaphysic. We have tried to avoid doing so thus far, in order, if not altogether to preclude controversy—for it is not possible to obtain universal consent and unanimity on even a single proposition, however plain, unmistakable, and simple it may appear —still to avoid dubitable and debatable points as much as possible. But longer to shirk this is to leave the subject in hand disjointed and unsupported.

The Self has been stated to be the first and most indispensable factor of life. It has also been stated that, in the conscious condition, the Self is always in a state either of Pleasure or of Pain. By careful examination it appears that Pleasure is the feeling of an expansion, an increase of the Self. The very essence of Pleasure is an enhancement of the Self, its growth, its intensification, its superiority over others or over its own past states, its *moreness* in short—moreness than before and as compared with others. These two comparisons, on analysis, come to mean the same thing, for the size, the measure of a Self at any particular moment must be a matter of comparison with others; so that, when we say "superiority over or moreness as compared with its own previous condition," we still implicitly compare it with others at least in the time of the previous condition in order to fix the size of that previous condition.

So Pain is the feeling of contraction, narrowing, inferiority, *lessness* of the Self than before and than others.

This seems to be as near an approach to a universally correct definition of Pleasure and Pain as is available.

But if Pleasure and Pain are capable of such uniform characterisation, how is it that in the concrete, in actual life, what gives pleasure to one Jíva gives positive pain to another, and *vice versa?* Do these facts contradict the definition or are they reconcileable with it? They are of course reconcileable with it; indeed it is out of all these facts that the definition has been generalised. The explanation is this.

It has been said before that a Jíva is a compound of the Pratyagátmá, the abstract Self, the One, and a portion of the concrete Not-Self, the Múlaprakṛiti, the Many. Not till such a combination takes place is the multitudinous process of Saṁsára possible. Self as such, the abstract Self, is incapable of being added to or subtracted from; It has no quantity It is only a unity. The Not-Self as such, the concrete many, is also incapable of being added to or subtracted from, for want of motive; it has no quality. In order that there should be any movement, quantity and absence of quantity must enter into relation and so produce quality; the Many and the One have to be transfused into each other; there must be a mutual superimposition—अध्यास *Adhyása*—of the two, each upon the other.

Where, however, the Self has become identified with an Upádhi, a portion of the Not-Self—when a Jíva proper, a conglomerate of the Self and Not-Self, the whole behaving and regarding itself as an individual—and thus a particular Self, a personality, has been formed, then contraction and expansion, pain and pleasure, become possible. And according as the nature of the particular, limited, individual personal Self is, so will be its cause of pleasure and pain. Whatever helps to expand that particular nature will be pleasurable, the opposite painful. Herein lies the explanation of so-called morbid pleasures and pains. When the Self happens to have become identified with a diseased condition of the Not-Self, then appears the mysterious phenomenon of pleasure—positive pleasure for the time being, however false and illusory otherwise—being caused by what actually promotes and perpetuates the disease and the feeling of the disease.

In view of the above remarks, for the purposes of the subject in hand Jívas may be divided into two broad classes. According to the general Law of Evolution and World-process, during the first half of a cycle the tendency is for the Self to identify itself more and more completely with the Not-Self, to fall more and more deeply into matter, as it is sometimes described, to become more and more separate by means of immersion in more and more concrete and mutually-resistant forms. The reverse is the case during the second half, when the Self dissociates itself more and more from the Not-Self and tends more and more to revert to its abstract unity. During the former period, accordingly, the period of the प्रवृत्तिमार्ग *Pravritti-Marga,* the path of action and engagement in the world, the causes of pleasure and pain are respectively those that expand or contract the material, the concrete, the separated Self, the lower Self, or rather the Not-Self that has assumed the mask of the Self. During the latter period, the causes are those that enhance or narrow the spiritual, the abstract, the united Self, the higher Self, the Self that has assumed the mask of the Not-self.

It should be remembered here that this is all a matter of grades and degrees, of relativity, of more and more, and less and less only; there is no complete, absolute loss of the instinctive feeling of unity (which is the result of the presence of the Self) on the first half of the cycle; as there is no complete, absolute loss of the instinctive feeling of separateness (due to the presence of the Not-Self) on the second half to its very end in Pralaya and Peace. The complete absence from manifestation of the one means the similar complete absence of the other, and the consequent collapse of the World-process into Pralaya for the time being; and thus it is that during manifestation Love and Hate are to be always found touching each other, from the very beginning unto the very end, though of course their power and prevalence vary in the two stages even as the height of the two ends of a see-saw might vary.

The result of all this is that during the first half of every cycle, large or small, representing the life of one human being or of a nation, a race or humanity, a world or a kosmos, the separative Emotions on the side of Hate and vice prevail. The greed for gain, for self-assertion, for individualism, for adding to one's own Upádhi at the expense of others is strong then, and Jívas predominantly belong to the class which is best described by the word "selfish." Later on, during the other half, when the power of the Not-Self decreases, the Self is recognised as separate and distinct from the Not-Self and as *One* in all Selves, all Jívas, then the Emotions that make for union, those on the side of Love and virtue, gather strength and Jívas belong to the class "unselfish." The pleasure-seeking youth becomes the self-sacrificing parent; a conquering nation or race becomes the civiliser and uplifter of subject-races rather than their exterminator; an orb or kosmic system gives away its own life and constituent material to a younger orb or system instead of swallowing up its compeers and brothers as Mártanda, the Sun, did in his younger days.

[This law, it should be noted, is true only as a general law, in the case of the typical cyclical life. In practice there is such an infinite commingling of larger and smaller cycles, each being at a different stage, and the cases of special protection and guidance of and consequent absence of evil amongst early races, and of violent distortion from the ordinary path, of disease and premature death, amongst individuals as well as nations during certain other periods of the life of humanity, are so common in consequence of other minor laws, that it may well appear to the casual observer that there is no such general Law governing the World-process. The Saṁskrit saying is useful to bear in mind in this connection:

यश्च मूढतमो लोके यश्च बुद्धेः परं गतः ।
द्वाविमौ सुखमेधेते क्लिश्यत्यन्तरितो जनः ॥

"He that is the dullest of the dull, or he that has attained to That which is beyond the Buddhi: these two only are the happy in the world; the midway Jívas are the unhappy."]

Selfish Jívas, as just said, find pleasure in whatever increases their material Self, their physical possessions and belongings; hence with them "taking" is the watchword of action. With unselfish Jívas, on the other hand, "giving" is the guiding principle. Because, in the one case, the Jíva feels that the more he solidifies his material Upádhi the more he strengthens, perpetuates, and expands his Self; while in the other he feels that the more he gives away of his Upádhi, the more he attenuates and thins it, the more the possibility of his Self uniting with other Selves, the more its expansion and increase.

In consequence of subtle modifications, however, which take place inevitably, a "taking" comes sometimes to be a taking in Love; it is accompanied with the desire to *repay* by grateful service, and hence has still the element of "giving" in it, and therefore belongs to the side of unselfishness and unity (*vide* analysis of "Devotion" *supra*). On the other hand, very often is "giving" a giving in unwillingness; it is then a "loss" and is accompanied by the wish to *take back* at the earliest opportunity. Such giving belongs to the side of selfishness and separation.

Bearing in mind the possibility of endless such modifications—all of which will be found capable of reduction by the general principles stated above—we may see that to one class of Jívas the circumstances arousing the one class of Emotions will be exclusively pleasurable and the opposite painful, whereas amongst the other exactly the reverse will be the case; that it is so happens by the invincible necessity of conditions. In every scene of actual life wherever there is occasion for the exercise of an Emotion of the one class there is present also, either as cause or as effect of the first-mentioned occasion, an occasion for an Emotion of the opposite class. This will be treated of later in dealing with illustrations of the character of literature.

It should be noted, meanwhile, that the desire of the Jíva is always towards "moreness" and away from "lessness." It loves that which makes it more; it hates that which makes it less. But the *it* which is to be made more or less is very different in different cases. *Desire* itself as such may well be said to be neither pleasurable nor painful. *That which is desired* to be gained, and the condition of the Self when it has been gained are called pleasurable. *That which is desired* to be avoided and *the condition* of the Self when it is not avoided are called painful.

(*c*) THE ESSENTIAL OBJECT AND CHARACTER OF LITERATURE.

Every desire is always accompanied by two pictures in the imagination, of its fulfilment and of its defeat. The provision of pleasurable pictures, representations of pleasurable emotion-feelings, of *Rasas*, is the business of all Poetry and Literature proper but, of course, what may be *Rasa* to one person may be *Kúrasa* (evil *Rasa*) to another ; and this is unavoidable.

The *form* of the poetry is allowed scant importance in the Indian science, though, in the West, metre, and to a less extent rhyme, have been held to be essential. Bain, and J. S. Mill before him, apparently approximate to the Indian view, which allows of such famous prose-poems as *Kádambari*, *Vásavadattá*, &c., and of course includes the drama under poetry at large, as one of its species. Walt Whitman and his imitators also recognise in practice the accuracy of this view. It may be, however, that this view is correct only in principle and as a theory. In practice the powerful additions made to the pleasure of poetry by metre and rhyme have considerably checked the growth of prose-poems and have thrown into the shade all but the very best. For similar reasons, just as the metrical poem is an advance upon the prose-poem, so recited poetry and the drama constitute an advance upon the metrical poem. To the musical effects of metre and rhyme which enlist the services of the ear in furthering the pleasure of poetry, the drama adds the scenic effects which engage the eye also. The mental picture of the desired *dénouement* (referred to before) is, in the drama, made the vividest that is possible without actually passing into the real. And hence the dictum **काव्येषु नाटकं श्रेष्ठं**—"Amongst poems, the drama is the highest." For similar reasons, too, it is that dance and song of man and woman in company represent the culmination point of esthetic enjoyment, of pleasure, of "moreness," that is known to present humanity

Form being thus discounted, it remains true that the primary business of literature, of all poetry, fiction, drama, and in a certain sense of biography, history, and narratives of travels also, is representation of Emotion-feelings (as distinguished from Emotion-desires) in their infinite combinations and permutations as actually or potentially present in multifarious human life. A nation's literature is in truth that nation's instinctive effort to provide for each of its members vicarious experience of the Emotion-feelings of all its members in all its manifold variety of life—even as a world-process is nothing more nor less than a vast endeavour to provide for its constituent Jívas direct experience of all possible pleasures and pains (corresponding to and being the actuals of Emotion-feelings), of all kinds of pleasures and pains possible within the spatial and durational limits of that particular world-system.

This also helps to explain how those writers come to be regarded as the greatest, and those works become the most permanent and the most prominent, that have seized and embodied the most permanent and prominent Emotion-feelings of humanity in the most remarkable manner.

So true is this that if the mental constitution of a race, a nation, be changed, all its literary idols and ideals would be replaced also. This truth is in fact embodied in all the trite expressions about change of fashion, change of taste, &c. Such expressions indeed appear trite only because applied to small and common matters. They are none the less true, and, in their full significance, important. What is true of the small is also true of the great. The histories of nations, the histories of races, the vast story of humanity as a whole—all are illustrations of changes of taste and changes of fashion. The inner life of the Self seeks ever new forms and ways of expression, expression of Emotion-desire and realisation of Emotion-feeling; and it is possible and instructive to read the stories of the different nations as the stories of the workings of single ruling Passions and Emotions. But the basic Emotions—Love and Hate, Benevolence and Pride of heart, Humility and Fear—these persist throughout, however great the changes of taste as to the subtler combinations of them. They are understood always, at all times, in all places, and the great epics of the nations shall be always read and always honoured because they comprehensively grasp and powerfully depict these basic Emotions. The subtler shades and combinations of them, on the other hand, elude the grasp of the general public, excite a temporary and evanescent interest, and remain confined to the few that by courtesy are called "the poets of poets" of each time and cycle.

(d) ILLUSTRATIONS.

The *Rasas* most common in the extant literatures of the world are, according to the Indian Science of Poetry, eight in number: (1) The Beautiful and Erotic; (2) the Comic; (3) the Pathetic; (4) the Heroic; (5) the

Furious and Cruel; (6) the Fearful; (7) the Disgusting; and (8) the Sublime and Wonderful. A ninth *Rasa*, शान्त *Shánta*, the *Rasa* of Peace and Renunciation of the world, is sometimes added to the list; but it is a *Rasa* in a negative sense only, by opposition as it were to the *Rasas* proper whose gradual abolition constitute the interest of the *Shánta*. The *Rasa* itself in actual life is to be found in all countries and times; wherever man has lived he has known frustration of desire, and the finer natures, *i.e.*, the older or more advanced Jívas of every race, have drawn Vairágya and Shánti and renunciation of the world from such frustration; but the poetical representation and embodiment of this Emotion has been largely confined to India.

The perusal of the above list at once gives rise to the question why poetry and literature allow a place to *Rasas* like the Furious, the Fearful, the Disgusting, and even the Pathetic. Why is it true, in the words of the ancient Indian poet, रसेषु करुणो रसः "The highest of the *Rasas* is Pathos"; and in those of the modern English singer,

> Our sweetest songs are those that tell of saddest thought.

Why should there be such amazing outbreaks

of the Horrible, the Disgusting, and the Cruel in the literature of the nations? Men desire only the pleasurable Emotion-feelings. And are not these painful ones? and if so, why are they cultivated?

The answer is to be found in all that has gone before, mainly in what has been said above regarding morbid pleasures and pains, in the fact that these outbreaks in literature correspond with outbreaks in actual life.

The so-called "painful Emotion-feelings" are (1) either not painful at all, but positively pleasurable to the class of Jívas that seek them for their own sake; or (2) the scenes corresponding to them are necessary backgrounds for the play of the opposite Emotions.

It has been said just now that with every Emotion-desire goes an Emotion-feeling, and that every Emotion-feeling is accompanied by two pictures in the imagination, one of the fulfilment of the desire and the other of its defeat. The former is pleasurable, and the latter only painful. And if this is so, it is easy to see how every Emotion-feeling that does not precede actual realisation in life may remain pleasurable.

Emotion-desires may loosely, and not accurately, be called pleasurable or painful in this sense, that the one set takes its rise in pleasure and the other in pain. In actual life the Emotion-feelings corresponding to the latter Emotion-desires are also painful. The painful picture is the most prominent in them; it is no longer imaginary; it is *expected*; the imagination has passed there into the more dense form of inference and expectation.

The Fearful.—An unarmed and defenceless man in the presence of a tiger feels the Emotion-desire of Fear—the desire to run away, to escape, to put distance and separation between himself and the animal. The Emotion-feeling here is purely painful, because the picture of the fulfilment of the desire is very weak indeed, while the other picture, matter of expectation as just said and not of imagination, is overpoweringly strong.

But let the incident occur not in real life but in a tale that we are reading. Now two kinds of "Selves" generally appreciate a story of danger and adventure. The actively timid spirit on the one hand, and the actively proud and strong spirit on the other. It looks like a contradiction in terms to say so, but he who has followed and seen reason to agree in the classification which ranges Pride and Fear in the same line, will easily see the truth of this also. The timid spirit contemplates the danger, the cause of Fear, and finds congenial occupation, interest, excitement, and expansion in devising plans to run away from the danger and avoid it. The pleasurable Emotion-feeling to it consists in the picture of successfully running away from the danger. This is the explanation of the fondness of children for blood-curdling stories, stories of ghosts and goblins and monsters and wild beasts, which make them shiver in ecstasies of fright. But in all these cases the enjoyment of the story and the eagerness for more of it would vanish at once if and as soon as it was realised by, really brought home to, the reader or listener that there was really no possibility of escape for him in a similar situation. In the other case, the proud and strong spirit also contemplates the danger, the cause of Fear, and finds congenial occupation, interest, excitement, and expansion in devising plans to avoid the danger; but his plans are to avoid the danger not by running away from it but by suppressing it. The pleasurable Emotion-feeling to him consists in the picture of successfully coping with and overpowering the danger in his own person in a similar situation.

Such is the explanation of the existence of the literature of the Fearful.

The Cruel and the Disgusting.—The explanation of the literature of the Cruel and the Disgusting is similar. Those that are in sympathy with the correspondent Emotions enjoy such literature and gloat over the destruction of the defeated enemy in full sympathy with the author of the cruel act, the murderer it may be, or the successful schemer and intriguer, or the adulterer, &c.*

The Pathetic.—Besides this, the opposite emotions also arise from the background of these. Thus "Pathos," "the Pathetic," is the counterpart of "the Terrible," "the Cruel," "the Disgusting," &c. The "sufferer" naturally goes along with "the author of suffering." In a scene thus involving the presence of both are therefore present materials for the sympathy of both natures, the virtuous and the vicious. The former, sympathising with the sufferer, experience the *Rasa* of करुणा : *karuṇah*, Pathos, Pity. Their Benevolence is strongly aroused, and the picture of the fulfilment of their desire to help is the source of their enjoyment of a tragedy.

Let us see what happens in such a case. In an Emotion of Benevolence, by psuedo-identification of the one, the superior, Jíva with the other, the inferior, Jíva, the former feels the pain of the latter. The desire arises in him to avoid

---

* Max Nordau's book on *Degeneration*, gives some apt instances of the outbreak of such evil Emotions in life and literature, even in times of peace. That they are very common in times of war is, of course, known to everybody.

that which is causing the pain, which is making the latter inferior, small, less. He forthwith tries to take away that which is causing the inferiority. The Self—wherein lies unity—being predominant in this relation, and the unity of the two being felt, there results inevitably the feeling of moreness and of pleasure, so far, to the superior; and the pain which is caused by the giving of a portion of the Upádhi (Not-Self) to the other to relieve his inferiority—though painful no doubt—is lost in the predominant pleasure. And, therefore, is "the quality of mercy doubly blessed." The superior feels the joy of the identification of the two selves; and the inferior that of the gain to his Upádhi and relief of positive pain. But let there be no doubt that to the material body, the Not-Self portion of the superior, the act of giving *is* a painful one. The mere fact of an unnoticed degree in small cases should not be allowed to hide the underlying truth which is recognised confessedly in all the associations of the word "sacrifice." That an act of Self-sacrifice is pleasurable is true only so far as the Self-portion of the Jíva is concerned; not as regards the Not-Self-portion. And in this last fact lurks the danger of much exercise of the emotion of the Pathetic out of actual life, which danger will be shortly referred to.

To return: while the action of adjusting the inequality is in progress, in fact as soon as the desire to associate with the inferior and lift him up arises in the mind of the superior, there also arises in his mind the picture of the end he seeks to secure and of what he seeks to avoid. The former being a picture of the completed "association" and therefore of gained "moreness" is pleasurable. The other is "painful." The former picture is sought to be realised in outer life, in action, in reality. The other is similarly avoided: so much so that people turn away from suffering they cannot help; it gives them pain only without any possibility of the pleasure of relieving it, and they cannot bear to see misery that is hopeless. This in actual life. But in imagination, in literature, whatever the end of the story, whether a completed tragedy or not, the imagination always contemplates the possibility of relieving the distress and so can find enjoyment.

When such an Emotion is called up in poetry by delineating the appropriate occasion and circumstances, the reader naturally, if his Jíva be so constituted as to be in sympathy with the subject (that is to say, if Benevolence be an Emotion congenial to his Self) pictures predominantly the pleasurable *dénouement* which he himself would create if he had the opportunity, and revolves it constantly in mind, exercising his benevolent propensities in all ways possible under the circumstances; and so he derives pleasure from the poetry. His "benevolent Self" is, so to say, intensified, made more, in the pictured *dénouement*.

But if he were not in sympathy with the subject, the poetry could have no charm, no interest for him; and if his Jíva belonged distinctly to the opposite class, then any expressions in the work calculated to evoke Benevolence or appearing to demand Pity would be positively painful to him, and he would only side with and enjoy the description of the deeds of the author of the suffering in the work.

But a great danger underlies the enjoyment of such scenes of pathos by even the benevolent and the full of pity.

There have been human beings who, originally virtuously inclined and taking pleasure in deeds of charity and help and service to others, having begun to take pleasure in mere tales or dramatic representations of such, and have gradually sunk into being contented with such imaginary exercise of their Benevolence. And they have fallen further, if their worldly position has given them the requisite power, into that awful condition of the apparently unintelligible human monster who, not content with imaginary scenes for his imaginary Pity, devises actual real scenes of cruelty and torture to human and other beings in order to excite and expand his "pitying Self." Lest this seem too far-fetched, consider the case of singing-birds separated from their mates and confined in different cages in order to make them sing more passionately and sweetly. The very commonness of the practice hides the subtle and refined cruelty underlying it; and it is no more noticed than the true significance referred to before of the fattening of animals for the slaughter-yard. Who knows but that the refined and cultured men that sat on the throne of decadent Rome, Caligula and Nero and their kin—who have been prominent in all nations in the days of their disruption, even as foul worms in a putrefying corpse; who were common in the mediæval ages of Europe as well as of Asia—who knows but that they have been really such aberrations of nature, not only wild savages, with merely the instincts of Hate predominant in them. These phenomenal Jívas seem to appear largely only at those stages in human history when a turning point is reached, when the Self and the Not-Self elements of the Jíva are both almost equally strong, when the struggle between them is the severest, when Pity is necessary to indulge in, and yet the pain of the sacrifice of the Not-Self, alluded to before, is so great as to prevent a real and true indulgence of it.

Of course, it may be that in any one or all of the particular instances referred to above, the Jívas were only purely vicious natures, in whom the element of Not-Self, and consequently the force of separation, were overpoweringly predominant, and who therefore took a pleasure in the cruel sights of the arena only to gratify their Emotion-desires of Hatred and Pride. But the other view is not altogether useless. It supplies a possible explanation in certain cases which are otherwise inexplicable.

And in that explanation, perhaps, may be found a reason why the science of the Indian drama tacitly discourages tragedy writing ; why tragedies, songs " Of old, unhappy, far-off things and battles long ago," " Sweetest songs that tell of saddest thought," Songs of the separation of lovers," belong not to the strongest and most vigorous stage in the story of a nation, but perhaps to the period of its weakness. The Indian view is so strong on this point that the author of the *Uttara-Ráma-charita*—than which it is not easy to conceive a finer study of Pathos in any language or literature—has given a happy ending to his work, directly contradicting even the traditional story of the sage Válmíki.

It is desirable in many ways that the valuable

Emotion of Pity should not be wasted on air. The literature and the scenic representation of the Pathetic should be only sparingly allowed, and used principally for the cultivation and development of the finer feelings, when such is deemed expedient and possible in view of the ever-present danger of arousing sympathy in a vicious nature with the evil characters of the drama. In the words of Ráma to his lifelong servant and ceaseless devotee Hanumán: 'I do not wish at all to pay thee back the kindness thou hast done to me: to wish this were to wish that thou shouldst be in pain and need my help: and such wish is the wish of the false friend and not the true." To be always *seeking in imagination*, *i.e.*, in imagined scenes of suffering, which is very different from prayer for the well-being of the world—for the gratification of one's benevolent propensities is to be always desiring that others should be in misfortune. So closely do good and evil elbow each other in human life and so difficult is it to distinguish between them always.

It is clear that (1) The Beautiful and Erotic, (3) the Pathetic, and (8) the Sublime and Wonderful belong to the side of Love and Attraction, while (5) the Furious and Cruel, (6) the Fearful, and (7) the Disgusting, belong to the side of Hate and Repulsion. The interest of (2) the Comic, and (4) the Heroic is mixed. The Comic consists of Ridicule and Good-humour; while the Heroic is similarly made up of Pride and Self-sacrifice.

(e) THE OTHER ARTS.

What is true of poetry and literature in that they are representations of the Emotions, is also true of painting, sculpture, music, architecture, and the other Fine Arts of the past and the future, with this difference; that in all these, in some more than in others, but still in all, the purely sensuous element, as distinguished from the emotional, is greater than in poetry and literature.

From what has been said above as to the nature of Emotion and as to the factors involved in it (ch. iii., iv., and ix.) it will have appeared that *Emotion* as distinguished from merely physical and sensuous craving, appears only between Jíva and Jíva. There is no Emotion between feeder and food, seer and colour as such, hearer and sound, smeller and scent—though each of these objects may be intensely pleasing or painful. It is only when "subjects" become "objects" to each other that complicated relations arise, intellect is born, and multifarious forms of action in social and national life, trades, commerce, governmental institutions, come into being—all three, Intellect, Emotion, and Action increasing in complexity side by side, and language too growing correspondingly.

Poetry and literature are therefore, as is generally and naturally recognised, the means of the completest and closest exposition of human life. The other forms of art sometimes do not aim at representing or arousing Emotion in this sense at all—a landscape, a sea-scene, a wordless melody may appeal to the purely sensuous consciousness, and may be "beautiful" only as pleasing exclusively to the eye or the ear. But this happens seldom: a "human interest" is generally given to his work by the author; he introduces elements which arouse Emotions of love, or sympathetic Fear, or Pathos, or Heroism. Even architecture is either "devotional," or "grand and sublime," or "stern and forbidding," or "strong and massive," or "dull and lifeless," and so forth. At the present stage of humanity, combinations of Sense and Emotion are the most attractive and the most appreciated. That music is the most honoured which is not only pleasant to the ear but also expresses an Emotion powerfully, either by suggestion and association or directly by appropriate words, and so far is poetry. That sculpture, that painting, receives the most praise, which is not only faultless as a masterpiece of form or colour, but also embodies a powerful Emotion with which the beholder's temperament is in consonance.

CHAPTER X.

THE IMPORTANCE AND PLACE OF EMOTION IN HUMAN LIFE AND THE SOURCE OF ITS POWER.

Bearing the facts set forth above in mind, it is not difficult to see that all life is only an unfoldment of the possibilities of Emotion-desires and Emotion-feelings. Every page, every paragraph, every sentence of every book of literature directly embodies a phase of emotion. And it may be said in a certain sense correctly, that such is the case with even every book of science, though indirectly, for the direct object of such is the collection of cognitions and not the representation of Emotions. Very instructive exercise is it for students to try to specify these phases of Emotion. For literature is only a representation of actual life, more or less accurate. And every action, every movement, every spoken word of every individual human being, and again his whole life considered as a unity and in the man, will be found to represent one "ruling passion," if he be properly studied.

Even as a single atom acted on simultaneously by the motions of millions upon millions of other atoms has *one* motion which is the single resultant of all these numberless motions *plus* its own special motion, so the whole of every human life may be reduced to a unity of Emotion-desire and Emotion-feeling. And from this standpoint, as mere object of operation and study, each life, each phase of Emotion, stands on a level with all others. The picking and choosing amongst them comes later. For the time, the student only sees that Emotion-desire stands at the very centre of life; immediately directs all actions and movements whatsoever as means of its own gratification; and indirectly guides the collection of cognitions, the acquisition of knowledge, as means to the proper performance of those actions.

From this standpoint, the life of an emperor of continents, the history of a conqueror of nations, the path of a Teacher of the worlds, is on the same level with the life of a nameless beggar, of a long-forgotten victim of proud tyranny, of the most ignorant of the ignorant. Each represents one of the infinite phases of the abstract Self, the Pratyagátmá, in relation with the Not-Self, the Múlaprakṛiti.

That such and such a particular one of all these phases looms most largely before the gaze of a nation or a race at any time and place is only part of the arrangement by which each phase gets its due turn. So long as humanity is double-sexed it will remain true that:

> All thought, all passions, all delights,
> Whatever stirs this mortal frame,
> All are but ministers of Love,
> And feed his sacred flame.

It is the same with other Emotions. There comes a time in the life of every Jíva when the Self insists on exercising its omnipotence in the startling phase of the power of suicide, of denying and killing itself, when it says: "Only the Not-Self is; only matter is; there is no such thing as I, as the Self, the spirit; eat, drink, and be merry, for to-morrow we die." There comes another time when it runs to the opposite extreme of belittling and denying the Not-Self, and says: "There is no such thing as matter at all; no such thing as Not-Self; all is spirit, all is I;" and it adds: "Take no thought for the morrow," drawing the same conclusion from infinitely different premises—the truth as ever lying between.

Thus phases of Emotion have their reign and dominance in human story by turns, and the literature of the day reflects them.

But apart from this general importance of

Emotion in life, what is the special source of its power in particular instances, what is the special food on which Emotion-desire nourishes itself and grows overpoweringly strong so as to sweep away reason—on ever so many occasions in life? This food is imagination. It has been generally remarked that imagination is an essential factor in all the more remarkable forms of Emotion. Thus, there is no horror where there is no imagination: an actual battle-field with thousands slaughtered is not so horrible as a mysterious murder. The reason of this is to be found in the very nature of Emotion as explained in chapter iii. and the laws which govern its provocation as stated in chapter viii. An Emotion is a desire *plus* an intellectual consciousness. Where the desire does not find immediate vent in action, it works in and round the intellectual consciousness, as expectation, as imagination, and thereby gathers strength in the manner described in p. 130 of chapter ix. But that strength is, because of the very manner in which it gathers, not real, true, and enduring strength; and when sought to be utilised in action it very often fails. This is very noticeable in much modern urban life. Because of the increase of intelligence life has become largely emotional—in theosophical terminology, the astral consciousness is developed highly—and immense amounts of misery and happiness are gone through by human beings for causes purely airy—as they would be called from the standpoint of the physical body. A very slight physical matter, some careless piece of behaviour or management of affairs, entirely unimportant and trivial in itself, is made the basis of a large amount of imagined pleasant or painful situations and consequences and resulting pleasantness or unpleasantness. It should be noted that *some* basis, however slight, in physical conduct is absolutely indispensable. The attempt to separate Emotion and hold it apart altogether from Sense is as futile as the endeavour to give a value to money apart from the things it can purchase. As the true use and destiny and fulfilment of the latter is purchase of articles, so the true fulfilment of the being of the former is wholesome, righteous vent in action in actual life. The non-recognition and non-realisation of this essential fact is the reason why so very frequently Platonic loves begun with high ideals gradually descend into hysterics and idiocy, or worse still into sexual immorality and crime; and large fortunes commenced to be accumulated for comforts and ease of life end in mere miserliness and avarice.

The power of "soulful" eyes, the source of many a young person's distractions, of eyes "pensive and melancholy," of glances "fascinating" or "weird" or "serpent-like," of looks "suggestive" or "speaking whole volumes," is exactly this, that they are "suggestive" of indefinite possibilities, and "speak whole volumes"—but when required in actual daily domestic life to throw all these "suggestions" and "speeches" into actualities, they naturally often fail woefully and false expectations are properly disappointed. A single copper has often sufficed to build a castle, but only in the air; it will not buy one meal in common life.

As to what the significance is, from the point of view of evolution, of the endeavour to withdraw the Emotions from the senses, the endeavour to live in the Emotions rather than the senses, when such an endeavour is extensively observable in a large class of humanity, *e.g.* in an excess of imagination and literature over action—that significance seems to be that that class is seeking *new senses* in which to vent its Emotions, the present ones having grown stale; that biological changes in the physical constitution of the race are pending.

Notice in the current literature at the end of the nineteenth century how the sex problem is being threshed out from all points of view, and how its sensuous and actual side is being thrown more and more into the background by the mere Emotion-feeling element; how the feeling of ennui and weariness is spreading more and more; how there seems to be steadily growing, amongst men and women of culture and intelligence, a sense of disappointment and dissatisfaction with the present order and arrangement of nature. If this sense of dissatisfaction and weariness were to grow sufficiently strong and extensive, then it is conceivable that after the lapse of ages, after many relapses into the old conditions and temporary revivals of satisfaction and pleasure in them, radical changes in the physical constitution of man and his surroundings might come about, and humanity go back again through the bi-sexual to the asexual condition, with corresponding entire modification of the details—not the essentials—of intellectual and emotional constitution also—as some of the ancient books teach us.

CHAPTER XI.

THE HIGH APPLICATION OF THE SCIENCE OF THE EMOTIONS.

What is the practical application of the Science of the Emotions, a very brief exposition of which has been attempted? How may this knowledge be utilised for the bettering of human life?

To whom the Science is addressed.—What is true of all other knowledge is true of this. We know, and we strive in accordance with, and with the help of, our knowledge. But between the knowing and the striving there intervenes the wish for the object which is to be secured by the striving. Between the cognition and the action there interposes the Emotion, the desire, that connects the two. So to connect the knowledge of the science of the Emotions with the action for the improvement of humanity there is needed the real, earnest, true wish to improve one's own life and that of others. Otherwise the science is useless, as a looking-glass unto the blind. Perhaps worse than useless. The unscrupulous may wrench it to suit their own evil purposes.

This wish cannot be forced. It must be left to come of itself. To what has been said before as to the broad division of Jívas into two classes, and of the passing of each Jíva from the one into the other class, it should be added that the wish *must* come to each Jíva at some time or other in the course of its evolution, when that Jíva ceases to live for itself; when after a period of Vishâda and Vairâgya and blankness, in which—still with a remnant of that purest selfishness which is the very beginning of unselfishness—it seeks for peace and rest and quiet for itself, it realises that Peace, and realises in that same moment also that it *has* to live for others by the supreme Law of the World-Process, which compels it to repay in love to others what it has itself received by love from others; when the एषणात्रय *Eshaṇa-traya*, the threefold seeking—for पुत्र *putra*, वित्त *vitta*, and लोक *loka*, for progeny, wealth, name, and place in the world; for perpetuation and expansion of the Self in children, in material possessions, and in the mind and opinion of the world—which led it into the incurring of the ऋणत्रय *Ṛiṇa-traya*, the three-fold debt—to the Pitris or ancestors, the Rishis or the teachers, the Devas or the Gods, who severally give progeny, mind and knowledge, and worldly possessions—is reversed, and forces it to gird up its loins to discharge the *Riṇa-traya*; when it sees the truth of what Kṛishṇa said:

एवं प्रवर्तितं चक्रं नानुवर्तयतीह यः।
अघायुरिंद्रियारामो मोघं पार्थ स जीवति ॥

"He that helpeth not to maintain revolving the wheel of the cycles thus set going, but seeketh the pleasure of his own senses and liveth in sin, he liveth in vain indeed, O son of Pritha."

The reason why such time must come to every Jíva must be sought in the Metaphysic of the World-Process—of its How and Why. It is enough to say here that in that time of Vairágya and desolation, which comes on the Jíva when the desire that guided it onwards down the प्रवृत्तिमार्गः *Pravritti márgah*, the Path of Action,* fails and dies, all Sensations and Emotions—the highest, noblest, grandest, dazzling and enchaining the mind, or the lowest, vilest, meanest, disgusting and revolting it—are all, without one single, solitary exception, seen to be on the same level, seen to be mere empti-

* The Path of Action is the path of attachment to, of engagement in, of pursuit of, the material life, the arc of the descent into matter, as opposed to the Path of Renunciation, the निवृत्तिमार्गः *Nivritti márgah*, the arc of ascent into spirit.

ness and dream. In that time all the old motives fail, because the very fount of all such motives, the desire for experiences, is exhausted. But the one motive, the one desire, if it may be so called, remains, viz., the desire for Self-preservation, for Self-understanding. This desire is the instinctive grasping by the Self of Its own immortality in Its abstract, Pratyagátmá, aspect. Such is the supreme Love and Compassion of the Self for the Self that It always blesses Itself, मानभूयासं, *Mánabhúyásan*, "May I never not be." Out of this desire rises inevitably, necessarily, without fail, the understanding of the universal nature of the Self. This *understanding* is the essential liberation of which a great One has said: "Moksha is not a change of conditions but of condition."

After the coming of such time is the Science of the Emotions mostly helpful. The Jíva cannot fully understand and realise the true meaning of Love and Hate, till he has in some moment or other of his life risen beyond them both into, and preserves the memory of, the region in which neither has existence and from which both take their birth. But having once seen them in their bareness and essence, having realised how all the Emotions are on the same level from a certain standpoint, the Jíva can thenceforth delibrately choose those on the side of Love—it is impossible for him to choose otherwise after such vision of Truth—for the use of humanity.

From that time onwards, with ever clearer vision, the Jíva looking before and after, understanding the way he has come, understanding also the way he has to go back, knowing the nature of the desire that led him forwards, knowing the nature of the desires that are holding him—the Jíva rises above them by that very knowledge, for to know is to be above and beyond that which is known; and day after day he uses them for the good of others, throwing off a fetter every now and then from his own limbs or from those of another, knowing that he cannot rid himself or others of all at once, until the final Peace is gained at the end of the destined world-cycle.

True it is what Krishna said:

अहंकारविमूढात्मा कर्ताहमिति मन्यते ॥

"The Jíva enwrapped in Ahamkára (the feeling of a separate Self), thinketh 'I am the doer.'"

True also is His riddle:

प्रकृतिं यान्ति भूतानि निग्रहः किं करिष्यति ॥

"All beings follow their nature; what shall restraint avail?"

But the truth is not as so many interpretations put it—an advice to feel a hopeless helplessness in the presence of a crushing, irresistible, and relentless Fate, an advice to follow blindly the instincts and impulses of one's lower nature, whether good or evi.

Such is not the truth. The truth is that the statements are an explanation, and not at all a direction. Wherever the feeling of "*Aham*" of I, a Self, an Ego, is, there also is the feeling of "freedom," of "power to act." If the latter is an illusion, it is only because the former is an illusion too. Just as the separate Self is a reflection, in a mass of the Not-Self, of the united, the abstract Self, the Pratyagátmá, so too and in the same degree, is the feeling of free-will a reflection therein of the "unlimitedness," the non-limitation of that Pratyagátmá. The two go hand-in-hand. It is not right to say "I am," and at the same time also to say "I am compelled absolutely by something else than I." The *whole* compels all parts equally. The *whole* does not *compel* any one part by preference, nor does any one part compel any other absolutely, and compulsion equal for all is compulsion for none. The **निग्रहः** *Nigrahah*, restraint, in the shloka, means restraint by one weak part exercised against another stronger part of, and not the whole of, Prakṛiti. For restraint is also part of Prakṛiti. And advice

mand, *are* addressed and should be addressed only where the possibility of their proving effective, of their being listened to and followed, is already in the bud. Were it not so, advice and instruction had long been abolished from this world. The truth underlying them is that he to whom they are addressed, however outwardly impervious and adverse to them, has in him, by mere fact of being human like him who addresses them, the possibility of the wish to follow them.

Thus then may the Science of the Emotions be addressed to all, though all may not now obviously and openly be in sympathy with its practical purpose. For, hidden away in the heart of each member of the human race, is the seed of Vairágya. And there is no mystery in this. Desire is in the human heart. And desire carries with it its own frustration, and in the frustration is Vairágya.

Cultivate Vairágya, then, my brothers and my sisters! and when the seed of it begins to show soft sprouts within your minds, nourish and guard them carefully. Cease to live for the separated Self; begin to live for others. There is no fallacy in spreading broad this counsel, friends! For though it has been said just now that there is that in every human heart which is potentially pervious to this counsel, yet only in a very few has that seed germinated so far that the water of this counsel will help it to grow.

There seems to be an inconsistency herein; thus: there is the possibility of Vairágya and of living not for the separated Self but for others in the heart of every Jíva, and so this counsel to live for others may be addressed to all. But there is also the impossibility of *all* living for others, and so an impropriety in directing the counsel to all. The explanation of the inconsistency is this: that what is impossible simultaneously is perfectly possible in succession; all may live for others, not at the same time, but successively.

In the majority the seed of Vairágya is yet lying asleep; it has not found the soil and the season in which it may awake and grow. Long yet must they continue to live for the separated Self in the course of the Law. This science and this counsel will not reach their ears, or if their ears then surely not their hearts. Their turn will come much later, and when it comes the "endless flow of Máyá" will have provided other Jívas for whose good these later comers will be living then.

And, listening to the counsel, what remains to do? The outer life of him who has thus achieved the true intelligence, is कृतबुद्धि *krita-buddhi*; who has seen and is full of the Self,

आत्मवान् *átma-ván*; nay, who has made his Self, created it anew, regenerated it, is कृतात्मा *kritátmá*—his outer life will be the same as that of all good men, only more good, more self-sacrificing. For is he not deliberately living now for others, while the ordinary good-hearted man is obeying the inclination of his heart unconsciously, under the dictates of the special past karma which connects him with those to whom he does his service?

Such a man becomes, by constant practice, the master of his Emotions from having been their slave; and by and bye he learns to guide the Emotions of his fellow-men also into the better ways. And so he can preserve his calm unshaken always, doing all his duties with a mind at perfect peace, unagitated, undisturbed by anything, and so pass on from stage to stage of evolution till the end in Peace.

Human Life.—What are the stages through which the Individuality of the Jíva grows and passes?

We are told that in the evolution of a Jíva there are three unvarying stages. (1) The stage of consciousness—very latent and unmanifest it may be, as in the mineral or vegetable condition, or massive and gregarious and racial, as in the herds of lower animals, or separated and strong, as amongst the lower human races. (2) The stage of self-consciousness—when the Self is more or less distinctly felt as different from the body and from other Selves, and is treated as such implicitly; when it is distinctly recognised as a *one*, as an individual, amongst many ones and individuals, as in the more advanced classes of humanity. And (3) the stage of All-Self-consciousness, when the Self is recognised as one in all Selves, as in Those who have gone beyond humanity.

Through these three stages, the One, Pratyagátmá limiting itself into separate individuals, is always returning again to Its original unity in the illusion of the World-Process.

In practice, these stages of the Jíva's evolution are accomplished by means of different and distinct kinds of material bodies, the number and density of which apparently differs with different world-systems.

In our own system it seems that in the earlier forms, which we call the lower and the grosser, the Jíva líves entirely in the outer sheath. Its thought is identical with its desire, its desire identical with its action. Its life is constant actions, constant movements of the physical body. It reaches out at once for whatsoever it desires, however passingly; it runs away as

without the slightest pause, the least deliberation, without thought in short. This is the purely physical stage.

By and bye, when separateness—"manyness"—increases between the growing Jívas, conflicting desires and aversions move each Jíva simultaneously. The consequence is a deadlock in the physical body and great activity in the Jíva, which begins to realise itself as separate from the body, regarding the latter as an instrument, as something belonging to it, in short, as *its* and not as *itself*. But how can the Jíva be separate and active without an Upádhi, a sheath? Forthwith it begins to utilise more largely the subtler astral body, and as it progresses this is formed of finer and finer matter.

Indeed, as copies of copies of copies may be made *ad infinitum*, so consciousness and imagination may draw further and further inwards and go further and further outwards *ad infinitum*. The more outwards they go, the greater the sense of separateness and mutual resistance, the denser the matter; the more inwards they recede, the less the sense of separateness and mutual resistance, the finer and subtler the matter.

So, again, with a still more extensive growth of manyness and separateness and much complexity and multiplicity of desires and aversions, when the Jíva comes to see and feel that the entertainment of even these desires and aversions is pleasant or painful—when it comes to cognise the nature and aspects of *Rasa*—then the *desires* come to a deadlock, and the Jíva picks and chooses from them deliberately. The literary stage, the increase of mind in the sense of the lower intellect, results. The careful following out of the consequences of desires and aversions, and of actions in accordance with them, expands the lower intelligence enormously (if as yet un-self-consciously), and great intellectual results, in social life, in trade and commerce, in literature, physical science, and the arts, proceed from this stage of the Jíva's life. The Jíva, in order to pick and choose between desires and aversions and connected actions, has to organise for itself another and still finer Upádhi, called the mental body.

By and bye the processes of the lower intelligence, the mind, become so complex, so extensive, so multifarious, that the Jíva becomes tired of them, and has to pick and choose between them. Its constant and increasingly intense struggles with others throw it back again and again on itself, and the Self-consciousness of the Kárana-Sharíra, or causal body, arises at this stage. But the Self-consciousness is the consciousness of the *individual separate* Self. And this is a very subtle and strong body and hard to transcend. The *Ahamkára*, the "I"-ness, is sublest and strongest at this stage, and in conjunction with a highly-developed mental body and intelligence there appears within it the phenomenon of "desires being desired." The real thing desired is of course the material object of the desire, and not the desire itself; but with the excessive and lopsided development of the Intelligence (the characteristic of the 5th race) and the exhaustion of the ordinary Sensations and Emotions, we see that phase of life which is described as the "craving for Sensations and Emotions," the "craving for a great Love, or a great Hate," "the blankness and craving due to the absence of a motive."

This stage of Self-consciousness, concentrated into utter isolation and blankness, naturally and immediately precedes the next, wherein the life of the individual separated Self is seen to end in pain only, where pleasure was expected and desired. At this stage arises that *unlimited* Vairágya*, which is based on the pain and despair born of separateness, of manyness itself.

And then the Jíva recovers its lost memory of Oneness. A remnant, however, lasts of its

---

* *Vide* The *Yoga-Vásishtha* (Mumukshu-Prakarana).

separateness and individual existence. The return journey may not be accomplished in a moment when the outward journey has occupied so many ages and æons. This remnant, combined with the Jíva's new insight and belief, builds the buddhic body; still an individual separate body, but *seeming* to work in a way almost entirely the reverse of that of the former bodies. While former ones reached *out* from the one to the others around, this seems to reach *in* from the all around to any particular one, the process corresponding to the process of the highest and the truest Metaphysic. And yet this is not in reality so. The inversion of the point of view causes this apparent inversion of method of action also. Inasmuch as the essential nature of all action, all movement, is the same, and there is no action or movement possible without limitation and separateness, the inversion is only apparent, and due to extreme rapidity of motion, and the preponderance of the All-Self-consciousness over the mere Self-consciousness. Where formerly the Jíva thought: "How may I benefit myself at the expense of others?" and looked out from one point towards his surroundings, his circumference, he now places himself at the circumference, grasps in consciousness the whole sphere of the kosmos, of which he is a part, and from that standpoint looks in at any particular Jíva-point that is requiring help, and thinks: "How may I, the whole, benefit this, the part?" The touch of separateness and illusion that now exists is the *Sáttvika*, the pure, part of Avidyá.

As the All-Self-consciousness becomes overpoweringly predominant there results the nirvánic or átmic body, and still beyond come the still higher inconceivable stages of consciousness and bodies lasting to the end of the activity and the commencement of the pralaya of the particular kosmos we are concerned with.

Such is the evolution of the Jíva and the growth of his Individuality. Individuality is "memory and expectation centred in *a one*." The longer that one can look backward into the past and forward into the future, the stronger is the individuality. The more constantly one can preserve the memory and expectation, the clearer one's higher consciousness of unity with the Pratyagátmá, the *finer* that individuality The growth of the individuality corresponds with the growing refinement of the encasements. It should be remembered that in the case of each of these encasements it is as much a "body" as the "physical," in the sense that it is still *material*, still made of Múlaprakṛiti, still different from the inner aspect of the Jíva, the Pratyagátmá;

and the names given to the bodies indicate only that that particular aspect of Pratyagátmá which gives the name is the most predominant and prevalent in that body. It does not mean that that *aspect* forms the *material* of the body. Jíva is Pratyagátmá from the mineral stage to the nirváṇic; its Upádhi is Múlaprakṛiti from the mineral stage to the nirváṇic. So, too, the three aspects of the concrete, individual Jíva, viz., Gnyána, Ichchá, and Kriyá—knowledge, desire and action; correspond to the three aspects of the abstract, universal Pratyagátmá—Sat, Chit, and Ānanda; as also the three aspects of the concrete, individual Upádhi, viz., Dravya, Guṇa, and Karma (substance, attribute and motion), correspond to the three aspects of universal Múlaprakṛiti—Sattva, Rajas, and Tamas; these also persist from the lowest to the highest.

Many problems are cleared up by this view of the growth of individuality. Many a crystal, many a flower, many an animal, in its perfection, is far more beautiful than a sickly human child; many a human child is far more beautiful than a sickly human youth or weak old man. And yet each succeeding one of the list looms larger in our mental perspective than the preceding ones; and we unconsciously, instinctively, welcome its growth and preservation, or regret its loss and destruction accordingly. This is due solely to the fact of a successively larger and firmer individuality.

Let us, then, strive to grow the buddhic body and the buddhic consciousness, and let the lower bodies take care of themselves; or rather, indeed, let us try with all our might to rise above them once for all; and so when they in their due course—for the Jíva must pass through them unavoidably—take definite form, still they shall not be strong to hinder us and delay our journey onwards in the process of evolution.

There is no impossibility in this. At the great turning-points of cycles the Jíva catches a glimpse of *all* the future stages, and he may attach himself deliberately to a distant one rather than a nearer, regarding his necessary passage through the nearer ones—for he cannot altogether overleap and avoid them—as only a temporary necessity and means; or he may attach himself to a nearer one, when he will have to pass through the turning-point of Vairágya again and again before he gets hold of the next goal. In exact proportion to the stretch and extent of his Vairágya is the Jíva's stride of progress in evolution.

It may be that the outer circumstances of the majority of students are not favourable to conduct and life such as are required by a developing buddhic consciousness. But all can try to approach to an ideal, perfecting their consciousness and their conduct side by side. By constantly maintaining the breadth of the consciousness so as to include all; by always regulating conduct so as to seek in love the good of all; these are the means whereby the buddhic consciousness and body are developed and at last perfected. And in helping towards such perfection lies the true use of the Science of the Emotions.

How Human Life is Helped by this Science.— We have seen how the very root of all the virtues is the Emotion of Love; how the very Essence of Love is the realisation of the unity of all Jívas; how this realisation is the very heart of the Higher Consciousness. To those who have passed through the vast toil of the mental journey through the wildernesses of doubt and the deserts of despair is now secure the reward of being able to deliberately and consciously cultivate and compel the growth of Love in the soft and fruitful soil of their minds by persistently feeding it with the waters of the perennial stream of that Truth, the unity of all Jívas. To others who have not undergone this labour, Love is only an instinct, a flickering and fitful flame, uncertain, doubtful, to be lit by passing pleasures and extinguished by passing pains; burning stronger and longer in some natures, dying down quickly in others, and, by reaction, leaving behind more strong the foul smell and smoke and darkness of Hate. And also, to these others, Love is an instinct in and of the Upádhi, the Not-Self, the separated Self, the mere reflection of the true Self; such Love too is therefore only the reflection of the true Love, and it is invariably and in its deepest hiddenness the love of the *personal* Self, the *separate* Self, and therefore never free from the taint and the danger of latent selfishness. But once the Truth of truths has been clearly seen, the flame has been lit for ever, and, though it may and will be weakened now and again, it can never entirely die out; and the Love so compelled to grow is the *impersonal* Love, the love of the united Self, a Love that always turns its face towards and is always reaching out to, the abstract Pratyagátmá, and so *cannot* be limited and selfish.

Feeding then this flame of Love constantly with the oil of that great Truth, we can see and secure for the use of ourselves and of all humanity all the gems and jewels of the other virtues. So, bearing ever in mind the untruth of the manyness of Jívas, we can forcefully, untiringly, struggle against Hate and all its band of vices. Knowing the true nature and essence of Emotion-desire, we can watch every thought and word and action of our own in the constant light of Self-consciousness and Self-analysis, and those of others in the light of All-Self-consciousness, whereby we see that the desires of all are as the desires of each. And so watching, and knowing that whatever of us and from us causes pain and hurt and harm to another is due to our *desire* to live for our separate Self, to foster our own Ahamkára, to gain something for ourselves at the expense and pain of our brother —even though the gain be the merest fleeting feeling of pleasure, an Emotion-feeling, a Rasa, of pride or scorn—so watching and so knowing we shall avoid falling again into the power of desire, which has so long tied us to re-birth, which is the cause of so much misery to humanity, which has, no doubt, already been defeated in the great struggle of the period of of Vairágya, but which yet lifts again and again a rebellious and treacherous head, seeking for opportunity to regain and re-assert its sovereignty.

Knowing too the correspondence of the Emotions, knowing how they create in ordinary humanity—as fire does in ordinary combustibles—their own likeness, we shall be able deliberately to avoid creating in the minds of our fellow-beings any of the Emotions on the side of Hate and Vice; we shall be able to create in them the Emotions on the side of Love and Virtue.

When we see Fear, we shall not show the counterpart of Fear, *i.e.*, Scorn; we shall behave not as the ordinary combustible, that itself flames up at the touch of a flaming substance, but as gold that melts and becomes the purer the more it is exposed to the fire; we shall respond with Benevolence and tender Pity to Timidity.

When we meet with Pride and Disdain we shall not respond with Fear, as will the common weak nature, or with greater Pride and Scorn as will the common strong nature, but with Humility; and so responding with Humility, we shall transmute the other's Pride into Benevolence—for in ordinary humanity, to which most possessors of Pride belong, the counterpart of Humility is Benevolence—and thus we shall create in the other's mind a noble Emotion which will uplift him and be of use to others who need his help, though we ourselves may not need his Benevolence.

Or if we are not sufficiently masters of ourselves to force Humility upon ourselves in response to the other's Pride, and our nature, partaking overmuch of the common strong nature, surges up with the consciousness of our own superiority; then, at the least, we can add Love to that consciousness of our superiority, and transfuse the whole into a quiet Pity and Benevolence for the other's ignorance and Pride and Superciliousness. But let us remember that this is *not* the best way, but dangerous; for it may foster Pride in our own inner heart, and the Pity may become a sneering Pity instead of true Benevolence. For very subtle are the workings of Ahamkára and its manifestations. Let us guard against them carefully in ourselves by the only means of constant Self-watchfulness, and imperceptibly but powerfully we shall help others who come into relations with us to guard against them in themselves.

Do not let us laugh very often or very loud. There are more grounds for sorrow than for laughter in our present world. The great Teachers have laughed but seldom or not at all. Laughter *means* a sudden and excessive feeling of superiority and moreness, as explained before. People often laugh in Scorn. We are no longer actuated by Scorn. "But they laugh in Joy and pure Good-humour too, as it is called. May we not laugh with them?" Let us analyse that Joy and that Good-humour, and then determine for ourselves. Very often that Joy means the Joy of gain at the expense of another. "Even in jest?" we ask. Yes. The laughter of jesting consists in this: that one person *makes believe* that he himself is superior and another is inferior; this is done to bring out fictitious points of his own superiority and those of the other's inferiority, and so to secure a laugh. This "laugh at another's expense" is harmless, or supposed to be harmless, only so long as it is understood that the whole is a make-believe and that there is no real superiority or inferiority on either side. But apart from the merits or otherwise of so making-believe, and approaching falsehood even in jest—we see how often jest passes into earnest, and why? In trying to bring out the points of inferiority of others, people too generally pass from the fictitious to the real and touch sore parts; and the result is that the laughter rapidly changes from the humorous into the bitter. Let us not go near such dangerous shallows. What sad mistakes arise in life between the nearest friends! Expressions and gestures of Sympathy and Goodwill are mistaken for the very opposite. How great the danger, then, of the Self-assertion involved in even the laughter of jesting becoming hurtful.

And for reasons similar to those which make jesting and laughing dangerous, are also much talking and discussion dangerous. Let us ask a question when we really require some information; let us listen attentively to the reply, ponder it carefully, and ask again, if necessary. But why should we expound our own views uncalled-for? The danger of Self-assertion is there. But, if we are desired to state our views on any question, then we may certainly do so, if we can help another thereby, giving our statements in the way of the answers we ourselves would seek if putting questions. Because of the danger of Self-assertion and Ahamkára hiding within much speech, is silence golden.

As said before, the great Ones seldom laughed. But they have smiled very often: smiled in tenderness and sadness: sad to see another's pain, tender to relieve it; smiling because of their ability to do so, or at the unreality of the pain and its fleetingness; and, in any case, smiling because of the increased "moreness" of their own Self instantly acquired by the recognition of their identity with the Self of the person before them. As a general rule, the violent outward physical laugh is the laugh of the gross sense of the moreness of the material separated Self; while the quiet, tender, inner, spiritual smile is the smile of the subtle sense of morenesss of the spiritual united Self. And yet there is inevitably a touch of comparison in the purity of the latter also; a comparison of the strength of the united Self which has overpowered and transcended the strength of the Not-Self, the separated Self; and it is this comparison which—being misinterpreted naturally as invidious by the evil natures in which the separate-self is strong—causes the hatred of "spiritual faces" which is unhappily not an uncommon phenomenon amidst present humanity.

Let us distinguish well between this smile of tenderness and the smile of bitterness or of despair, wherein the Self snatches, it may be, a fictitious consolation for actual present loss from its own imagined greatness and another's littleness. And so distinguishing, we shall see why

> Manners are not idle, but the fruit
> Of loyal nature and of noble mind.

We shall not waste our time, our energy, and our new higher nature in meaningless and objectless reveries and imaginations. They are the कषायः *kaṣhdyah*, sourness, and the रसास्वादः *Rasásvádah*, sweets of imagination, that the Yoga warns us against. How often we discover with a start that we are imagining all sorts of situations of Anger and Discord between ourselves and those who are, or ought to be, most dear to us! We imagine them behaving wrongly to ourselves, and we revenge ourselves upon them by behaving equally wrongly to them in return—also in imagination! The real reason is that an unguarded and unrestrained element of evil Emotion in us has taken advantage of some very slight and small discomfort, and has run away with the whole of our mind, subdued it and turned its powers to its own uses. If we are pained in any way, and fail in a moment of carelessness at once to check off that pain as an item of past karmic debt cleared off, to welcome it as a piece of service done to another, then the Ahamkára-consciousness asserts itself, bases a desire for separation—an Emotion of Anger and Hate—on that pain, the mind begins to work in the imagination, and we at once find ourselves in the midst of all kinds of disagreeable scenes. And persistent failure in this respect confirms and condenses the imaginings into physical action with all its grievous results. This is how by assuming enmity we create enmity.

Allied to this is the mistake of openly attributing to a person an evil Emotion against which he may be struggling with might and main. His struggle and resistance against that Emotion cease at once and he breaks down, thinking it is useless for him to struggle, for others have decided that he has failed. As said before, by action and reaction, ever taking a new starting point in the last outbreak of the other person, the Emotions between man and man go on perpetuating their own endless flow. Wise are they that fix one starting point, and so enable themselves to close the accounts.

Thus, knowing the root of Desire, knowing that it is of the nature of the separated Self, knowing that we have no separate Self, we shall not fall a prey to such Desire-Emotions, and to such imaginings and mistakes. But on the contrary, as far as may be, we shall give credit even where none is due in strictness; for, by exactly the same process as that just described we shall thus create in the mind of the other that which will be really worthy of credit.

And as we shall avoid imaginings on the side of evil Emotion, so also we shall avoid much useless imagining on the other side, for the reasons set forth in the preceding chapter in connection with the Philosophy of Poetry.

But we shall cultivate assiduously to the best of our ability, Compassion and Pity, and the other virtues laid down for the Yoga-student, and herein make use of a chastened and ennobled imagination so far as it is helpful.

Thus steadfastly guiding our evolution, life after life; pure and serene, for ourselves and, so far as may be, for all those who are our fellow-passengers upon the road of evolution and have been bound to us by the bonds of karma; bearing ever in mind that "there is no purifier like unto knowledge"; fixing our gaze constantly upon the Eternal; living in the Eternal; realising that "nothing that is out of the Eternal," nothing that is less than the Eternal, "can aid us"; treading ever more and more firmly in the onward journey; seeing ever more and more clearly all in the light of the Self; may we hope to pass into the Final Peace, into the perfect realisation of the Paramátmá, in which are both Pratyagátmá and Múlaprakṛiti.

यस्त्वात्मरतिरेव स्यादात्मतृप्तश्च मानवः ।
समदुःखसुखो धीरः सोऽमृतत्वाय कल्पते ॥
नमोक्षो नभसः पृष्ठे न पाताले न भूतले ।
सर्वाशासंक्षये चेतःक्षयो मोक्ष इति श्रुतेः ॥

"The man of serene mind that rejoiceth in the Self and is contented therein, to whom pleasure and pain are as one, he becometh fit for immortality."

"Moksha lieth not hidden on the back of the heavens, or on the surface of the earth, or in the depths of Pátála; the dissolution of Ahamkára on the disappearance of all desire—such is Moksha as the Scripture sayeth."

LAST WORDS.

My reader! Never again, after having read this booklet with understanding, can you be altogether without the Self-examining consciousness and the Self-mastery that makes you turn again and again upon yourself to watch and regulate what you are thinking, saying, doing; and even if with this there should come upon you a harassing weariness and sense of emptiness of life and constant defeat of pleasure, you will not think that this is due to your new habit of Self-analysis. You will know that this has come to you with the partial cessation of Desire, which has made it possible for you to turn inwards towards the Self and understand the Science of the Emotions as one important portion of the Science of the Self. And you will know that it is this very Science that will help you to successfully struggle against and gain victory over that dreary emptiness and dull harassing weariness, by enabling you to cultivate Love universal and the capacity for work in identification with the life of Íshvara and gradually to find greater and greater joy in sacrifice for others, even as He finds joy in sacrifice for His worlds. Long do the uses of this

Science last—indeed, up to the very end of the kosmic system. For wherever and whenever is the Jíva-Self, there with it go its threefold activities of Cognition and Emotion and Action; and therefore always is it useful to know and bear in consciousness the inmost nature of these three. Facts of outer science are useful or useless according to the outer material surroundings. The chemistry of an element, the physics of a force, are useless in a world where that element or that force is not. But there are no worlds where Jívas are not; and therefore are the facts of inner Science useful always; therefore is the Science of the Self, *Adhyátma-Vidyá*, the highest of the Sciences.

ॐ शुभं अस्तु सर्वे जगतां
सर्वो भद्राणि पश्यतु
लोकाः समस्ताः सुखिनो भवन्तु ॐ

PEACE TO ALL BEINGS.

INDEX.